KING LEAR

William Shakespeare

Edited by
CEDRIC WATTS

WORDSWORTH CLASSICS

For my husband
ANTHONY JOHN RANSON
with love from your wife, the publisher.
Eternally grateful for your unconditional love.

Readers who are interested in other titles from
Wordsworth Editions are invited to visit our website at
www.wordsworth-editions.com

For our latest list and a full mail-order service, contact
Bibliophile Books, 5 Datapoint, South Crescent, London e16 4tl
tel: +44 (0)20 7474 2474 fax: +44 (0)20 7474 8589
orders: orders@bibliophilebooks.com
website: www.bibliophilebooks.com

First published in 1994 by Wordsworth Editions Limited
8B East Street, Ware, Hertfordshire sg12 9hj
Newly-edited text, new introduction and notes added in 2004

isbn 978 1 85326 095 7

Text © Wordsworth Editions Limited 1994 and 2004
Introduction, notes and other editorial matter © Cedric Watts 2004

Wordsworth® is a registered trade mark of
Wordsworth Editions Limited

Wordsworth Editions
is the company founded in 1987 by
MICHAEL TRAYLER

Typeset in Great Britain by Antony Gray
Printed and bound by Clays Ltd, St Ives plc

CONTENTS

GENERAL INTRODUCTION

The Wordsworth Classics' Shakespeare Series presents a newly-edited sequence of William Shakespeare's works. The inaugural volumes are *Romeo and Juliet*, *The Merchant of Venice* and *Henry V*, followed by *Twelfth Night*, *Hamlet*, *A Midsummer Night's Dream*, *King Lear* and *Othello*. Wordsworth Classics are inexpensive paperbacks for students and for the general reader. Each play in the Shakespeare Series is accompanied by a standard apparatus, including an introduction, explanatory notes and a glossary. The textual editing takes account of recent scholarship while giving the material a careful reappraisal. The apparatus is, however, concise rather than elaborate. We hope that the resultant volumes prove to be handy, reliable and helpful. Above all, we hope that, from Shakespeare's works, readers will derive pleasure, wisdom, provocation, challenges, and insights: insights into his culture and ours, and into the era of civilisation to which his writings have made – and continue to make – such potently influential contributions. Shakespeare's eloquence will, undoubtedly, re-echo 'in states unborn and accents yet unknown'.

CEDRIC WATTS
Series Editor

INTRODUCTION

King Lear is widely regarded as Shakespeare's most intense, profound and powerful tragedy. To people reading or seeing it for the first time, it can seem dauntingly strange. It is variously realistic, archaic, grotesque, implausible, absurd, horrific, tempestuous, poignant and heart-rending. Vividly, it raises enduring questions about human nature, human suffering, morality, religion and life's significance. The literary modes employed vary from functional prose to passionate poetry, from doggerel verse to miraculously lyrical flights. Critics are usually reluctant to concede that in Shakespeare's greatest works we find incongruous mixtures of weakness and strength, but, in *King Lear*, both are amply present.

Any reader soon notices some conflicts between what the action requires and what the Jacobean stage permits. When, after dividing the kingdom, Lear visits Goneril, she complains that 'his knights grow riotous': apparently Lear has a retinue of 'a hundred knights and squires' who, she says, are wild and randy, devoted to 'epicurism and lust' . He replies that they always behave impeccably: they 'all particulars of duty know'. But, infuriated by her desire to reduce the retinue by half, he and his followers leave for Regan. Regan tells him to return to Goneril; but Lear says that she will only accept fifty followers, whereas Regan will take a hundred. Not so, says Regan: twenty-five should suffice; indeed, adds Goneril (who has joined her sister), why do you need even five? At this point, Lear, overcome by rage and grief, sweeps out on to the heath. Thus, to the reader, a big question is presented. Are Lear's followers riotous, as Goneril says, or well-behaved, as Lear says? But this leads immediately to the other question, where *is* this huge retinue? In Act 1, scene 4, Lear is attended, according to

the earliest text (1607–8), only by some servants; whereas, according to the 1623 text, he is there attended by an unspecified
number of knights. Certainly, thereafter, we see no large body of
armed supporters. When Lear visits Regan in Act 2, scene 4, he is
accompanied by the Fool and a retinue of one – either a single
knight or a single gentleman (as those early texts again differ).
Later, when Lear roams the heath, there is no sign of the large
retinue, even though (at 3.7.15–19) thirty-five or thirty-six
knights were said to be escorting him to Dover. Fair-weather
friends, perhaps, or incompetent map-readers? In the Prologue of
Shakespeare's *Henry V*, the speaker explains that the only way in
which the battles in France can be made plausible in the theatre is
for the audience to use its imagination: 'Piece out our imperfections with your thoughts.' In *King Lear*, in the absence of such a
frank admission of the disparity between what Shakespearian
staging permits and what the story suggests, the disparity is the
more glaring and confusing. We recall the small stage, the limited
budget, and the actors who were used to playing several rôles in
one production. The rapid absence of Lear's large – but necessarily invisible – retinue is made embarrassingly evident; and the
question about their conduct remains unanswered in the text.
(Peter Brook's film version, in 1971, filled the gap by showing
numerous riotously unruly followers: textual gaps are directorial
opportunities.)

Another example of the oddity of the plot is provided by
Gloucester's leap. It also illustrates Wilson Knight's argument that
in *King Lear*, tragedy is perilously close to bathos, absurdity and
grotesque humour.[1] Blinded and despairing, Gloucester seeks to
kill himself by leaping from an imagined cliff-top. (Usually, in the
theatre, Gloucester jumps forward a metre or so and falls down on
the stage.) Edgar, his disguised son, assures him that he has fallen a
huge depth and has been miraculously saved. 'Why I do trifle thus
with his despair / Is done to cure it', explains Edgar; and, for a
while (though not durably), Gloucester does seem determined to
bear his lot with patience. Nevertheless, the sequence has been
peculiar. 'Trifling with despair' seems to sacrifice plausibility on
the altar of contrivance. A far better cure for despair would have
been for Edgar to reveal himself to his father. (Indeed, Edgar
himself says that it was 'a fault' not to have identified himself

sooner.) But that would rob the plot of a number of twists and turns which culminate when Edgar defeats Edmund and at last publicly identifies himself. If you ask why the blind Gloucester wants to walk all the way to Dover Cliff to kill himself, the most plausible answer is structural: so that he can meet Lear, who has been directed to Dover, where Cordelia's forces are encamped.

Repeatedly, then, we find that odd conduct by characters has been solicited by plot-requirements. To put it more severely, Shakespeare has sometimes been unable to reconcile characterisation with the story. Perhaps the most important example is provided in Act 1, scene 1, when Cordelia's initial response to Lear's demand for a statement of love is so curt and legalistic as to provoke Lear's wrath. Elsewhere in the play, Cordelia speaks with warm sensitivity and tact; but, in that first scene, it is necessary that she should speak with provocatively resentful logic so that the subsequent plot, depicting the consequences of Lear's wrathful dismissal of her, can unfold more or less as it had done in the various sources available to Shakespeare. Of course Lear is wrong to set up so crazy a bargain with his daughters (so much land in return for so many declarations of love), but her response – 'I love your Majesty / According to my bond, no more nor less' – is asking for the trouble that the story-line requires. It's not surprising that that opening scene reminds us of folk-tale and fairy-story: Cordelia, Regan and Goneril may even bring to mind Cinderella and her two ugly sisters. Again, Edgar's initial gullibility (when Edmund advises him to hide from Gloucester), coupled with his readiness to flee instead of vindicating himself before his father, implies a weaker character than that displayed by Edgar subsequently; but that credulity is a product less of his personality than of the later plot-requirements. Gloucester himself helps the story along by his belief in the forged letter (though, in reality, Edgar would have communicated with Edmund orally) and by his ready acceptance of a travelling companion who is variously a madman, two different gentlemen and a yokel.

Some of the most remarkable breaches of realism (or, at least, of passably realistic consistency) occur when the Fool jokes at the expense of the audience in the theatre. At the end of Act 1, scene 5, for instance, when in the company of Lear and the gentleman, the Fool says:

> She that's a maid now, and laughs at my departure,
> Shall not be a maid long, unless things be cut shorter.

In other words, 'Any virgin in the audience who dares to laugh as I go off-stage will soon will be deflowered (unless penises are docked)'.[2] At the end of Act 3, scene 2, he offers the audience a recitation of prophetic doggerel, and surrealistically concludes: 'This prophecy Merlin shall make, for I live before his time': in other words, 'I cap my prophecy by telling you it isn't mine: in fact I prophesy that Merlin (the legendary magician who has not been born yet) will make it.' Nevertheless it has already been made – to the Fool's audience in the present time of 1605 or so. Shakespearian comic characters are often holders of the magical pilot's licence permitting them to travel through space and time. They thus anticipate those jokes in pantomime and in modern plays and films which depend on breaches of a fictional convention that is normally respected. (An example of such a breach: Groucho Marx, in the film *The Big Store*, turned to the audience and said of a villain, 'I could have told you in the first reel he was a crook'.) Even so, the prevailingly grim atmosphere of *King Lear* makes the Fool's banter with the audience seem oddly discordant. Not surprisingly, this banter is often cut from stage or film productions. A famous 'loose end' of the play is the mysterious absence of the Fool from Acts 4 and 5, though feminists may not regret this lacuna. Directors sometimes fill the gap by letting him be seen, a mute (or dying) observer, towards the end of the action. Like other Shakespearian works, *King Lear* is usually treated, in the theatre or the cinema, less as a text to be faithfully rendered than as a body of textual material to be cut and adapted as is thought desirable by the director and others involved in the production. (The disparities between the earliest printed texts suggests that similar adaptation was common in Shakespeare's day.)[3]

Of course, the Fool's reference to Merlin as a prophet in the future raises the question of the period in which the action of *King Lear* is supposed to be set. Culturally, the play's references are baffling. Characters invoke God, Satan, Adam and Eve, St Mary, churches and holy water: so the action may seem to belong to the Christian era. Yet the legendary Lear was a pre-Christian ruler, and characters also invoke 'the gods', Jupiter, Juno, Apollo, Hecate and Nature: so now the action seems to be located in a post-Roman but pre-Christian Britain. Other references (to Tom o'Bedlam, schoolmasters, spectacles, and fops who frequently visit the barber, for instance) suggest times virtually contemporaneous with Shakespeare's. So, culturally – and, above all, theologically – the story slithers about and sometimes is glaringly inconsistent. As Samuel Johnson remarked:

> Our authour by negligence gives his heathens the sentiments and practices of christianity . . . [He] commonly neglects and confounds the characters of ages, by mingling customs ancient and modern . . . [4]

Theological muddles were not unusual then: for example, in Thomas Kyd's *The Spanish Tragedy* (1592), a slain Catholic is judged by Pluto and Proserpine in the classical underworld. But, given the intense religious questioning within Shakespeare's play, in *King Lear* the muddle becomes more frustratingly prominent.

On the other hand, some parts of *King Lear* are expertly co-ordinated: notably various prominent themes and ironies. The story of Lear (or Leir) had been told by diverse writers before Shakespeare: notably, Geoffrey of Monmouth in *Historia regum Britanniae*, John Higgins in his part of the *Mirror for Magistrates*, William Warner in *Albion's England*, Geoffrey Holinshed in his *Chronicles*, Edmund Spenser in *The Faerie Queene*, and the author of the anonymous play entitled *The True Chronicle History of King Leir*. Shakespeare's great innovation was to link the Lear material with another story, which he had found in Sir Philip Sidney's *Arcadia*. That was the story of the King of Paphlagonia. This king has two sons, one legitimate and the other illegitimate. He is tricked by the illegitimate son, Plexirtus, into disowning the legitimate son, Leonatus. Subsequently, Plexirtus blinds his aged father and casts him out. Leonatus then serves as his guide in the wilderness, deflecting the old man from suicide, and with friends defeats Plexirtus and his men. The king dies after being fully reconciled with Leonatus, who inherits the throne.

Obviously, Shakespeare has used this story of the Paphlagonian king as the basis of the sub-plot in *King Lear* which involves Gloucester, Edmund and Edgar. By interweaving this with the

Lear story, Shakespeare has created a large number of parallels and thematic echoes. We now have two misguided fathers, and more than two instances of rivalry between siblings; twice we see a father being cruelly treated by a son or daughters; each father is exposed to the harshness of nature; and, in both cases, there is poignant reconciliation with the misjudged loving child. Lear may be 'a man more sinned against than sinning', but he has breached the morality of the family and the law of statecraft, and thus helped to bring his suffering on himself. Gloucester, too, had breached the morality of the family, by fathering Edmund during 'good sport' outside wedlock. Gloucester loses his sight; [5] Lear his sanity. Each has a disguised helper, 'Poor Tom' and 'Caius' respectively. During their wanderings, both men have remarkably similar moral insights. Lear says:

> Poor naked wretches, whereso'er you are,
> That bide the pelting of this pitiless storm,
> How shall your houseless heads and unfed sides,
> Your looped and windowed raggedness, defend you
> From seasons such as these? O, I have ta'en
> Too little care of this! Take physic, pomp:
> Expose thyself to feel what wretches feel,
> That thou mayst shake the superflux to them,
> And show the heavens more just.

Gloucester says to 'Poor Tom':

> Here, take this purse, thou whom the heavens' plagues
> Have humbled to all strokes: that I am wretched
> Makes thee the happier. Heavens, deal so still!
> Let the superfluous and lust-dieted man,
> That slaves your ordinance, that will not see
> Because he does not feel, feel your power quickly:
> So distribution should undo excess,
> And each man have enough.

The duplication (and even the word 'superflux' echoes in 'super-fluous') emphasises the theme: through suffering, people who were once rich and powerful may come to appreciate the needs of the poor and humble, and advocate charitable provision. This isn't socialism, it's *noblesse oblige*: recognition of the obligation of the nobility to be charitable. Both stories show a noble figure being reduced to hapless dependence on others; both juxtapose the formerly mighty with the lowly: Lear with the Fool, Gloucester with 'Tom'. The play is shot through with madness: the raging dementia of Lear, the deranged babbling of the supposed Bedlam beggar. The disguised Edgar appears now before Lear, now along-side Gloucester. The interweaving of thematic and ironic connections is deft; and the eventual meeting of the king with the blinded lord is one of the most telling in literature. 'O, let me kiss that hand!', says Gloucester. 'Let me wipe it first; it smells of mortality', is the resonantly ambiguous reply. Later:

> I know thee well enough: thy name is Gloucester.
> Thou must be patient. We came crying hither;
> Thou know'st, the first time that we smell the air
> We wawl and cry . . .
> When we are born, we cry that we are come
> To this great stage of fools.

In any good stage-production, it's a powerfully poignant scene; and the words can live on, outside their dramatic context, as memorable epitomes of human experience: 'What oft was thought, but ne'er so well expressed.'[6]

Critical discussions of *King Lear* often bear on the problem of theodicy. That is the problem of reconciling belief in divine justice with evidence of injustice here on earth. It is an ancient and continuing problem for religious believers, and it is the central issue in the long tradition of literary tragedies. If divine justice exists, why does it permit the existence of apparent injustice all around us? Why is it that good people often suffer, while bad people often prosper? *King Lear* seems determined to express this problem in particularly vivid, searching and harsh ways. Repeat-edly in the play, characters invoke or cite a variety of deities and metaphysical forces. Repeatedly there's a questioning of the entities that may govern our lives: are they kind, blind or cruel? Insistently, too, the play gives instances of the very kinds of suffering that make people seek some consolatory pattern in events. The suffering of Lear is painful enough; but the blinding of Gloucester is notori-ously horrifying ('Out, vile jelly!' – in the theatre it can still make people flinch and look away); and the death of Cordelia seems to

set the problem of theodicy with appalling starkness. Lear, referring to Cordelia as his 'poor fool' (which editors usually regard
here as a term of endearment), cries out in his misery:

> And my poor fool is hanged! No, no, no life!
> Why should a dog, a horse, a rat have life,
> And thou no breath at all?

It is a question which commentators often try to answer. Samuel
Johnson, in the 18th Century, found the death of Cordelia so
painful that he could not bring himself to read again the ending of
the play until his editorial duties obliged him to do so. He
contemplated sadly this text in which 'the wicked prosper, and the
virtuous miscarry': sometimes, alas, Shakespeare 'seems to write
without any moral purpose'.[7] Other critics have seen the play as an
affirmation of Christianity. G. I. Duthie, for example, in his
introduction to a Cambridge edition of King Lear, says:

> God overthrows the absolutely evil – he destroys the Cornwalls,
> the Gonerils, the Regans: he is just. God chastens those who err
> but who can be regenerated – the Lears, the Gloucesters – and in
> mercy he redeems them: he is just, and merciful. But again, God
> moves in a mysterious way – he deals strangely with the
> Cordelias of this world. His methods are inscrutable. Shake-
> speare presents the whole picture . . . This, however, can mean
> 'pessimistic' drama only to those who cannot agree that the play
> is a Christian play.[8]

If we seek guidance to Shakespeare's intentions by looking at his
adaptations of the various source-materials, a big paradox emerges.
His adaptations seem designed both to confirm and to subvert the
sense of divine ordinance of events.

As we have seen, his innovative addition of the Paphlagonian
material to the traditional Lear story provides duplications of
events and themes, and thus creates evident patterning; and evident
patterning implies a pattern-maker: we may infer some destinal
force at work within or above the action. That's the first half of the
paradox. The second half is well known. In all the surviving
previous versions of the Lear story (whether by Geoffrey of
Monmouth, Higgins, Warner, Holinshed, Spenser, or that anonymous playwright, or yet others), the story of the king ends

relatively happily. After his reconciliation with the virtuous daughter, he is restored to the throne and seems set to live happily ever after. Certainly, in several versions, the daughter eventually dies by suicide in prison after having been defeated in a rebellion by her nephews, but that happens a long time after the reconciliation: seven or eight years afterwards, according to Holinshed and Geoffrey of Monmouth. Only in Shakespeare's play does that daughter die *before* her father. Only in this play is the poignant reconciliation cruelly blighted by the sudden murder of the young woman. And only in this play does the king have happiness so abruptly snatched from his grasp as he receives the mortal shock of seeing the beloved child die. There was no precedent for the harrowing bleakness, the ruthless ironies and the harsh accidentality of the conclusion.

In Act 5, scene 3, the concluding scene, the reunited Lear and Cordelia are consigned to prison. Tenderly, Lear says:

> We two alone will sing like birds i'th'cage;
> When thou dost ask me blessing, I'll kneel down
> And ask of thee forgiveness.

There, he declares, they will enjoy many years in each other's company, blessed by benign gods. We soon learn, however, that Edmund has arranged for them to be killed. There follows much stage business, centring on the duel between Edmund and Edgar. At last, Kent enters to say farewell to Lear: 'Is he not here?' It's then that Albany exclaims,

> Great thing of us forgot!
> Speak, Edmund: where's the King? And where's Cordelia?

There's a flurried rush to send rescue. 'The gods defend her!', cries Albany. Then, as if in sardonic response to his plea for divine defence:

> *Enter* LEAR *with* CORDELIA *in his arms.*

So much for the 'judgement of the heavens' and the gods' guardianship.

In short, while some of the changes to the source-materials have increased the sense of the possibly providential ordering of events, other changes subvert that sense and emphasise an *absence* of

providential order. The exclamation 'Great thing of us forgot!'
(rather than, say, 'Great thing to be resolved!') forms part of that
subversion: accidentality and cruel ironies come to the fore. And
amnesia continues to accentuate the ironies. Kent kneels before
Lear, crying 'O my good master!'. Instead of recognition, the
response from the king is the uncomprehending 'Prithee away!'.
Edgar intervenes, trying to jog Lear's memory. ''Tis noble Kent,
your friend.' The appalling reply is: 'A plague upon you, murderers, traitors all!'. Lear is not only amnesiac; he sounds, for a
moment, every bit as wrathful and unjust as the Lear of the play's
first scene, long before his suffering and reconciliation. Next,
briefly, Lear veers into recognition of Kent, but promptly veers
away from lucidity again. As Albany observes,

> He know not what he says, and vain is it
> That we present us to him.

Nevertheless, Albany tries to make moral sense of the outcome:

> All friends shall taste
> The wages of their virtue, and all foes
> The cup of their deservings.

Yet it is then that Lear exclaims:

> And my poor fool is hanged!

– as if to say, 'Where are the wages of *her* virtue? How can
Cordelia's death possibly fit any pattern of moral justice?'

King Lear has sometimes been sentimentalised by critics who,
seeking some uplifting moral or religious doctrine within it, tend
to mute its jarring discords. If, on the other hand, we respond
frankly to its complexity, we find that it is a peculiarly jagged,
awkward, inconsistent and painful work which generates scenes of
immense power and searing memorability. If, at some times, we
become aware of the limitations of the Jacobean theatre, at other
times we recognise the awe-inspiring eloquence that that theatre
encouraged. In its conventions, the work shifts unpredictably
between the realistic, the self-mocking and the stylised. In its moral
concerns, King Lear reminds us of the human capacity for hatred,
cruelty and injustice; it also reminds us of the human capacity for
love and forgiveness. There are parts of the work which may

gratify the desire for moral justice (Cornwall, Edmund, Regan and Goneril perish); but there are also parts which mock that desire (Gloucester and Lear suffer appallingly, and Cordelia is killed). If Lear gains benevolent insights during his madness, he also vents misogynistic diatribes. If his sufferings are chastening, the effects are not durable. *King Lear* is often *sub*-tragic, in the sense that it hurls at us so rawly the messy stuff of human suffering that tragedies traditionally reduce to order. It may also seem *preter*-tragic (beyond it), in the sense that the play depicts human endeavours to impose patterns of moral significance on events which, arguably, resemble a muddle rather than a mystery. In *Troilus and Cressida*, Shakespeare suggests that when human beings deny divinely-ordained principles of co-operation, the result may be an *irrevocable* collapse of order. This may explain the structural paradox of *King Lear*: the combination of thematic harmonies and final discords.

Variously orderly and disorderly, clumsy and sophisticated, *King Lear* yet gives unparalleled poetic expression to a gamut of emotions: vituperative wrath, insensate indignation, demented wildness, penitential grief, bewildered timidity, loving forgiveness. Perhaps Shakespeare's intention was to use the variously ramshackle and elegant plot as the vehicle for searchingly eloquent expression of the paradoxes of human nature, ranging as that nature does between the extremes of hatred and love, madness and lucidity. Consider some of the most famous and oft-quoted lines:

> As flies to wanton boys are we to the gods:
> They kill us for their sport.

Or:

> Through tattered clothes great vices do appear;
> Robes and furred gowns hide all. Plate sin with gold,
> And the strong lance of justice hurtless breaks . . .

Or:

>   When the mind's free,
> The body's delicate; this tempest in my mind
> Doth from my senses take all feeling else
> Save what beats there . . .

Or:

> Unaccommodated man is no more but such a poor, bare,
> forked animal as thou art. Off, off, you lendings!

In the first example, there's a pessimistic view memorably
epitomised: it may not be generally true, but it sums up parts of
the play, and it also sums up the way life may appear at times of
adversity. Thomas Hardy remembered those lines, and they
reverberate in his darker novels. [9] The second example, declaring
'furred gowns hide all', vividly renders the notion that there's one
law for the rich and a harsher law for the poor: money masks
corruption. The third extract is a reminder of the play's graphic
rendering of physical and psychological suffering. And the fourth
offers one of many answers, suggested in the action, to the
question: 'What *are* human beings, basically?' Are we merely
'forked animals', our reality falsified by cultural trappings? Or are
we made human by social amenities? –

> Allow not nature more than nature needs,
> Man's life is cheap as beast's.

In short, the power of *King Lear* may lie less in any answers it
suggests than in its dramatic questioning of nature, morality, reason
and order, and in its eloquent voicing of a gamut of human
emotions. By virtue of intellectual scope and passionate intensity, it
remains Shakespeare's most challenging and formidable work.

NOTES TO THE INTRODUCTION

1 G. Wilson Knight: '*King Lear* and the Comedy of the Grotesque' in *The Wheel of Fire* (London: Oxford University Press, 1930; reprinted, London: Methuen, 1949).

2 An alternative reading is: 'Any virgin who deems this an exit in a comedy is so stupid that (unless penises are docked) she will soon lose her virginity.'

3 Illustrations of these disparities are provided in the notes towards the end of this volume.

4 *Johnson on Shakespeare*, ed. Walter Raleigh (London: Oxford University Press, 1908; rpt., 1957), pp. 159, 160.

5 Edgar explains the blindness thus to Edmund:

> The dark and vicious place where thee he got
> Cost him his eyes.

In David Lodge's novel *Small World* (London: Penguin, 1985), pp. 322–3, the critic Angelica says: '[We] are none of us, I suppose, likely to overlook the symbolic equivalence between eyeballs and testicles . . . ' (The hero, Persse, 'listened to this stream of filth with growing astonishment and burning cheeks'.)

6 Alexander Pope: 'An Essay on Criticism' (1711), lines 297–8. (I modernise the version in *The Works of Alexander Pope*, ed. John Butt; London: Methuen, 1963; p. 153.)

7 *Johnson on Shakespeare*, pp. 161–2; quotations, pp. 161, 20–21. Between 1681 and *circa* 1823, the version of *King Lear* which prevailed in Britain was Nahum Tate's. In Tate's happy ending, Lear and Gloucester are alive and well, while Cordelia prepares to marry Edgar.

8 'Introduction' to *King Lear*, ed. G. I. Duthie and J. Dover Wilson (London: Cambridge University Press, 1960; rpt., 1962), p. li.

9 See Hardy's 'Preface' (1892) to *Tess of the d'Urbervilles* (London: Penguin, 1985), p. 39; and 'Preface' (1895) to *The Return of the Native* (London: Penguin, 1985), p. 49.

FURTHER READING
(in chronological order)

Samuel Johnson: notes [1765] on *King Lear*, reprinted in *Johnson on Shakespeare*, ed. Walter Raleigh. London: Oxford University Press, 1908.

A. C. Bradley: *Shakespearean Tragedy*. London: Macmillan, 1904.

G. Wilson Knight: '*King Lear* and the Comedy of the Grotesque' in Knight's *The Wheel of Fire*. London: Oxford University Press, 1930. (This essay is also included in the Muir anthology listed below.)

Enid Welsford: *The Fool: His Social and Literary History*. London: Faber and Faber, 1935.

George Orwell: 'Lear, Tolstoy, and the Fool' [1947] in Orwell's *'Shooting an Elephant' and Other Essays*. London: Secker & Warburg, 1950. (This essay, too, is included in the Muir anthology.)

M. M. Mahood: *Shakespeare's Wordplay*. London: Methuen, 1957.

G. I. Duthie: 'Introduction' to *King Lear*, ed. G. I. Duthie and John Dover Wilson. London: Cambridge University Press, 1960.

F. E. Halliday: *A Shakespeare Companion 1564–1964*. Harmondsworth: Penguin, 1964.

Jan Kott: *Shakespeare Our Contemporary*. London: Methuen, 1964.

William R. Elton: *King Lear and the Gods*. San Marino, Calif.: Huntington Library, 1966.

Clifford Leech: *Tragedy*. London: Methuen, 1969.

Narrative and Dramatic Sources of Shakespeare, Vol. VII, ed. Geoffrey Bullough. London: Routledge & Kegan Paul; New York: Columbia University Press, 1973.

Samuel Schoenbaum: *William Shakespeare: A Compact Documentary Life*. London and New York: Oxford University Press, 1977; rpt., 1987.

Twentieth Century Interpretations of 'King Lear': A Collection of Critical Essays, ed. Janet Adelman. Englewood Cliffs, N.J.: Prentice-Hall, 1978.

The Division of the Kingdoms: Shakespeare's Two Versions of 'King Lear', ed. Gary Taylor and Michael Warren. Oxford: Oxford University Press, 1983.

Jonathan Dollimore: *Radical Tragedy*. Brighton: Harvester, 1984.

King Lear: Critical Essays, ed. Kenneth Muir. New York and London: Garland, 1984.

Kathleen McLuskie: 'The Patriarchal Bard' in *Political Shakespeare*, ed. Jonathan Dollimore and Alan Sinfield. Manchester: Manchester University Press, 1985.

The Cambridge Companion to Shakespeare Studies, ed. Stanley Wells. Cambridge: Cambridge University Press, 1986.

Alexander Leggatt: *Shakespeare in Performance: King Lear*. Manchester and New York: Manchester University Press, 1991.

New Casebooks: King Lear: William Shakespeare, ed. Kiernan Ryan. Basingstoke and London: Macmillan, 1993.

Brian Vickers: *Appropriating Shakespeare: Contemporary Critical Quarrels*. New Haven and London: Yale University Press, 1993.

Terence Hawkes: *William Shakespeare: King Lear*. Plymouth: Northcote House, 1995.

Russ McDonald: *The Bedford Companion to Shakespeare*. Basingstoke: Macmillan, 1996.

Kenneth S. Rothwell: *A History of Shakespeare on Screen: A Century of Film and Television*. Cambridge: Cambridge University Press, 1999.

Daniel Rosenthal: *Shakespeare on Screen*. London: Hamlyn, 2000.

John Sutherland and Cedric Watts: *Henry V, War Criminal? and Other Shakespeare Puzzles*. Oxford: Oxford University Press, 2000.

NOTE ON SHAKESPEARE

Details of Shakespeare's early life are scanty. He was the son of a prosperous merchant of Stratford-upon-Avon, and tradition gives his date of birth as 23 April, 1564; certainly, three days later, he was christened at the parish church. It is likely that he attended the local Grammar School but had no university education. Of his early career there is no record, though John Aubrey reports a claim that he was a country schoolmaster. In 1582 Shakespeare married Anne Hathaway, with whom he had two daughters, Susanna and Judith, and a son, Hamnet, who died in 1596. How he became involved with the stage in London is uncertain, but he was sufficiently established as a playwright by 1592 to be criticised in print as a challengingly versatile 'upstart Crow'. He was a leading member of the Lord Chamberlain's company, which became the King's Men on the accession of James I in 1603. Being not only a playwright and actor but also a 'sharer' (one of the owners of the company, entitled to a share of the profits), Shakespeare prospered greatly, as is proven by the numerous records of his financial transactions. Towards the end of his life, he loosened his ties with London and retired to New Place, the large house in Stratford which he had bought in 1597. He died on 23 April, 1616, and is buried in the place of his baptism, Holy Trinity Church. The earliest collected edition of his plays, the First Folio, was published in 1623, and its prefatory verse-tributes include Ben Jonson's famous declaration, 'He was not of an age, but for all time'.

ACKNOWLEDGEMENTS AND TEXTUAL MATTERS

With a title like that, this section may seem skippable; but the textual information here could be useful if you have to write an essay on *King Lear*, or if you face an examination-question about it, or if you are involved in a production of the play. The gist of the matter is that, from Shakespeare's day to the present, the text has been fruitfully variable, and will long remain so.

I have consulted – and am indebted to – numerous editions of *King Lear*, notably those by: Horace Howard Furness (Philadelphia: Lippincott, 1880; reprinted, New York: Dover, 1963); Kenneth Muir (the Arden Shakespeare: London: Methuen, 1952; reprinted, 1966); G. I. Duthie and J. Dover Wilson (London: Cambridge University Press, 1960; reprinted, 1962); G. Blakemore Evans *et al.* (*The Riverside Shakespeare*: Boston, Mass.: Houghton Mifflin, 1974); Stanley Wells and Gary Taylor (*The Complete Works*: Oxford: Oxford University Press, 1986); René Weis (Harlow: Longman, 1993); Stephen Greenblatt *et al.* (*The Norton Shakespeare*: New York and London: Norton, 1997); and R. A. Foakes (the Arden Shakespeare, 3rd Series: Walton-on-Thames: Nelson, 1997).

A 'quarto' is a book with relatively small pages, while a 'folio' is a book with relatively large pages. More precisely, a quarto volume is made of sheets of paper, each of which has been folded twice to form four leaves (and thus eight pages), whereas each of a folio's sheets has been folded once to form two leaves (and thus four pages). The earliest printed text of *King Lear* is the First Quarto (Q1), which was issued in 1607 and 1608. It is entitled: *M. William Shak-speare: HIS True Chronicle Historie of the life and death of King* LEAR *and his three Daughters. With the vnfortunate life of Edgar, sonne and heire to the Earle of Gloster, and his sullen and assumed humor of*

TOM *of Bedlam*. This version may have been based on Shakespeare's 'foul papers': i.e., an untidy manuscript. Various minor corrections were made during the course of printing, so that numerous surviving pages exist in both uncorrected and corrected states. In 1619, three years after Shakespeare's death, appeared the Second Quarto (Q2). This made some further corrections to Q1 but apparently did not use any independent manuscript. Then, in 1623, appeared the First Folio (F1): the first 'Collected Edition' of Shakespeare's works. The F1 text of *King Lear*, entitled *The Tragedie of King Lear*, differs markedly from the Q1 text. Q1 contains approximately three hundred lines which are absent from F1, while F1 contains approximately one hundred lines which are absent from Q1. Speeches are differently assigned; an entire scene is found only in the Quarto, as are Lear's 'mock trial' of his daughters and Albany's diatribe against Goneril; and there are hundreds of verbal variants, some trivial and some highly significant. The basis of the F1 text is a topic of scholarly debate and speculation, but one possibility is that the printers, while referring to Q1, used a copy of Q2 altered by reference to an independent manuscript, perhaps a prompt-book version. Whereas Q1 may derive from a script that existed before the play was performed, F1, with its substantial cuts, resembles a script which corresponds more closely to theatrical practice. (Successive printings of F1, as of Q1, incorporated various small corrections and changes.) Quite likely there existed a large and untidy quantity of *King Lear* material by Shakespeare which was revised, adapted and transcribed on various occasions. Shakespeare doubtless had second thoughts; censorship was a factor; and contemporaneous actors, audiences, scribes, prompters and compositors will all have influenced what has survived for us today.

The Quarto and Folio texts obviously represent different versions of one play, not two different plays. For many years, therefore, a standard procedure of editors was to conflate the two texts so as to produce a comprehensive new text. Eventually, however, Stanley Wells and Gary Taylor, when editing Shakespeare for Oxford University Press, felt that the textual differences were too great to justify such conflation. In 1986, accordingly, they published two versions of the play. The first, based on Q1, was *The History of King Lear*. The second, based on F1, was *The Tragedy of King Lear*. Nevertheless, Wells and Taylor did not follow a similar procedure for *Richard III*, *Romeo and Juliet*, *Henry V*, *Hamlet*, *Troilus and Cressida* and *Othello*, which also display marked differences between their Quarto and Folio forms. In 1989, Michael Warren produced a facsimile parallel-text volume of *King Lear*, and this was followed in 1993 by René Weis's non-facsimile *King Lear: A Parallel Text Edition*: in each, the Quarto and Folio versions were displayed side-by-side on facing pages. In 1997, *The Norton Shakespeare* went further, including *three* versions: *The History of King Lear*, *The Tragedy of King Lear* and (in a conflated text) *King Lear*. Meanwhile, Q1 was republished separately by Jay L. Halio in 1994 as *The First Quarto of King Lear* and by Graham Holderness in 1995 as *M. William Shakspeare: His True Chronicle Historie of the life and death of King Lear and His three daughters*. Collections of the Quarto and Folio texts could be consulted in, for example, *Shakespeare's Plays in Quarto*, ed. Michael J. B. Allen and Kenneth Muir (1982), and *The Norton Facsimile: The First Folio of Shakespeare*, ed. Charlton Hinman (1968).

There thus exist numerous editions which make evident the alternative materials of *King Lear*. Sometimes the Quarto material is superior, sometimes the Folio; and often they are qualitatively equal. In practice, in the theatre, most productions have used, and continue to use, a conflated text. Furthermore, the reader who surveys the differences displayed by, for instance, the Warren or Weis volumes, may well construct, in his or her imagination, a new *King Lear*, a unique synthesis. There are many options. Some readers may prefer the Quarto version of the play and some the Folio; but, as each version lacks important material unique to the other, many readers will prefer a conflationary, comprehensive text. The present Wordsworth edition offers a conflation: I have combined, as I think best, material from both the Quarto and the Folio, so that no important speeches are absent. The end-notes draw attention to particular textual problems and options, citing numerous differences between Q1 and F1. I have adopted various emendations offered by previous editors; and, as usual, the spellings and punctuation have often been modernised, while some stage-directions have been added.

In short, there is far more 'play' – flexibility, variability and adaptability – in *King Lear* than you might at first imagine. The opportunities for readers, critics, actors and directors are admirably numerous. One reason for Shakespeare's durability is that the divergences, ambiguities and puzzles in the early texts provide plenty of room for later variations, adaptations and interpretations. In Shakespeare's day, the script of this tragedy was evidently changing in response to diverse needs and pressures; and, ever since, it has repeatedly been transformed in the imaginations of readers and audiences.

I hope that the present edition of *King Lear* represents a practical compromise between the early texts, Shakespeare's intentions (insofar as they can be reasonably inferred) and modern requirements. In the interests of rhythm and euphony, I have occasionally retained archaic spellings which other editions modernise. For example, I have preferred Shakespeare's 'vild' to the modernisation 'vile', as loss of the 'd' weakens the alliterative pattern in such lines as 'Wisdom and goodness to the vild seem vild'. The glossary explains such archaisms and unfamiliar terms, while the annotations offer clarification of obscurities. No edition of the play can claim to be definitive, but this one – aiming for clarity and concise practicality – can promise to be very useful.

KING LEAR

CHARACTERS IN THE PLAY

LEAR, *King of Britain.*
GONERIL, *his eldest daughter.*
REGAN, *his second daughter.*
CORDELIA, *his youngest daughter.*
DUKE OF ALBANY, *husband of Goneril.*
DUKE OF CORNWALL, *husband of Regan.*
KING OF FRANCE, *suitor to Cordelia.*
DUKE OF BURGUNDY, *another suitor to Cordelia.*
EARL OF GLOUCESTER.
EARL OF KENT.
EDGAR, *elder son of Gloucester.*
EDMUND, *illegitimate son of Gloucester.*
OLD MAN, *Gloucester's tenant.*
CURAN, *Gloucester's attendant.*
FOOL *attending Lear.*
OSWALD, *Goneril's steward.*
DOCTOR *serving Cordelia.*
CAPTAIN *serving Edmund.*
HERALD.
MESSENGER.
KNIGHTS, SOLDIERS *and* TRUMPETERS.
GENTLEMEN, ATTENDANTS *and* SERVANTS.

KING LEAR

The throne-room in King Lear's palace.

Enter KENT, GLOUCESTER *and* EDMUND.

KENT   I thought the King had more affected the Duke of
          Albany than Cornwall.

GLO'STER It did always seem so to us; but now, in the division of
          the kingdom, it appears not which of the Dukes he
          values most, for qualities are so weighed that curiosity
          in neither can make choice of either's moiety.[1]

KENT   Is not this your son, my lord?

GLO'STER His breeding, sir, hath been at my charge. I have so
          often blushed to acknowledge him that now I am
          brazed to't.   10

KENT   I cannot conceive you.

GLO'STER Sir, this young fellow's mother could; whereupon she
          grew round-wombed, and had indeed, sir, a son for
          her cradle ere she had a husband for her bed. Do you
          smell a fault?

KENT   I cannot wish the fault undone, the issue of it being so
          proper.

GLO'STER But I have a son, sir, by order of law, some year elder
          than this, who yet is no dearer in my account. Though
          this knave came something saucily to the world before   20
          he was sent for, yet was his mother fair, there was
          good sport at his making, and the whoreson must be
          acknowledged. Do you know this noble gentleman,
          Edmund?

EDMUND   No, my lord.

GLO'STER My lord of Kent. Remember him hereafter as my hon-
          ourable friend.

EDMUND   [*to Kent:*] My services to your lordship.

KENT   I must love you, and sue to know you better.

EDMUND   Sir, I shall study deserving.   30

GLO'STER He hath been out nine years, and away he shall again.
          [*A sennet sounds.*] The King is coming.

Enter SERVANT (*bearing a coronet*), *then* KING LEAR, CORNWALL,
     ALBANY, GONERIL, REGAN, CORDELIA *and* ATTENDANTS.

LEAR   Attend the lords of France and Burgundy, Gloucester.
GLO'STER   I shall, my liege.   [*Exit.*[2]
LEAR   Meantime we shall express our darker purpose.
           Give me the map there. Know that we have divided
           In three our kingdom; and 'tis our fast intent
           To shake all cares and business from our age,
           Conferring them on younger strengths, while we
           Unburthened crawl toward death. Our son of
                                            Cornwall,   40
           And you, our no less loving son of Albany,
           We have this hour a constant will to publish
           Our daughters' several dowers, that future strife
           May be prevented now.[3] The princes, France and
                                            Burgundy,
           Great rivals in our youngest daughter's love,
           Long in our court have made their amorous sojourn,
           And here are to be answered. Tell me, my daughters
           (Since now we will divest us both of rule,
           Interest of territory, cares of state),[4]
           Which of you shall we say doth love us most,   50
           That we our largest bounty may extend
           Where nature doth with merit challenge?[5] Goneril,
           Our eldest-born, speak first.
GONERIL   Sir, I love you more than word can wield the matter;
           Dearer than eyesight, space and liberty;
           Beyond what can be valued rich or rare;
           No less than life with grace, health, beauty, honour;
           As much as child e'er loved, or father found:
           A love that makes breath poor, and speech unable.
           Beyond all manner of 'so much' I love you.   60
CORDELIA   [*aside:*] What shall Cordelia speak? Love, and be silent.
LEAR   [*pointing to a map:*]
           Of all these bounds, even from this line to this,
           With shadowy forests and with champains riched,
           With plenteous rivers and wide-skirted meads,[6]
           We make thee lady. To thine and Albany's issues
           Be this perpetual. – What says our second daughter,

	Our dearest Regan, wife of Cornwall? Speak.
REGAN	I am made of that self metal as my sister,
	And prize me at her worth. In my true heart
	I find she names my very deed of love;
	Only she comes too short, that I profess
	Myself an enemy to all other joys
	Which the most precious square of sense possesses,
	And find I am alone felicitate
	In your dear Highness' love.

REGAN   I am made of that self metal as my sister,
           And prize me at her worth. In my true heart
           I find she names my very deed of love;   70
           Only she comes too short, that I profess
           Myself an enemy to all other joys
           Which the most precious square of sense possesses,
           And find I am alone felicitate
           In your dear Highness' love.

CORDELIA   [*aside:*]   Then poor Cordelia!
           And yet not so, since I am sure my love's
           More ponderous than my tongue.

LEAR   To thee and thine, hereditary ever,
           Remain this ample third of our fair kingdom,
           No less in space, validity and pleasure   80
           Than that conferred on Goneril. – Now, our joy,
           Although our last and least, to whose young love
           The vines of France and milk of Burgundy
           Strive to be interested:[7] what can you say, to draw
           A third more opulent than your sister's? Speak.

CORDELIA   Nothing, my lord.

LEAR   Nothing?

CORDELIA   Nothing.

LEAR   Nothing will come of nothing;[8] speak again.

CORDELIA   Unhappy that I am, I cannot heave   90
           My heart into my mouth. I love your Majesty
           According to my bond, no more nor less.

LEAR   How, how, Cordelia? Mend your speech a little,
           Lest you may mar your fortunes.

CORDELIA   Good my lord,
           You have begot me, bred me, loved me. I
           Return those duties back as are right fit,
           Obey you, love you, and most honour you.
           Why have my sisters husbands, if they say
           They love you all? Haply, when I shall wed,
           That lord whose hand must take my plight shall carry   100
           Half my love with him, half my care and duty.
           Sure I shall never marry like my sisters,
           To love my father all.

LEAR	But goes thy heart with this?
CORDELIA	Ay, my good lord.
LEAR	So young, and so untender?
CORDELIA	So young, my lord, and true.
LEAR	Let it be so; thy truth then be thy dower!

LEAR   For, by the sacred radiance of the sun,
The mysteries of Heccat and the night,
By all the operation of the orbs   110
From whom we do exist and cease to be,
Here I disclaim all my paternal care,
Propinquity and property of blood,
And as a stranger to my heart and me
Hold thee from this for ever. The barbarous Scythian,
Or he that makes his generation messes
To gorge his appetite, shall to my bosom
Be as well neighboured, pitied and relieved,
As thou my sometime daughter.

KENT   Good my liege –

LEAR   Peace, Kent!   120
Come not between the dragon and his wrath.
I loved her most, and thought to set my rest
On her kind nursery. [*To Cordelia:*] Hence, and avoid
                         my sight! –
So be my grave my peace as here I give
Her father's heart from her. – Call France! Who stirs?
Call Burgundy! [*Exeunt two attendants.*] – Cornwall
                        and Albany,
With my two daughters' dowers digest the third;
Let pride, which she calls plainness, marry her.
I do invest you jointly with my power,
Pre-eminence, and all the large effects   130
That troop with majesty. Ourself, by monthly course,
With reservation of an hundred knights
By you to be sustained, shall our abode
Make with you by due turn. Only we shall retain
The name and all th'addition to a king; the sway,
Revénue, execution of the rest,
Belovèd sons, be yours; which to confirm,
This coronet part between you.

KENT	Royal Lear,
	Whom I have ever honoured as my king,
	Loved as my father, as my master followed, 140
	As my great patron thought on in my prayers –
LEAR	The bow is bent and drawn: make from the shaft.
KENT	Let it fall rather, though the fork invade
	The region of my heart! Be Kent unmannerly,
	When Lear is mad. What wouldst thou do, old man?
	Think'st thou that duty shall have dread to speak
	When power to flattery bows? To plainness honour's
	bound,
	When majesty stoops to folly. Reserve thy state,
	And in thy best consideration check
	This hideous rashness. Answer my life my judgement: 150
	Thy youngest daughter does not love thee least,
	Nor are those empty-hearted whose low sounds
	Reverb no hollowness.
LEAR	Kent, on thy life, no more!
KENT	My life I never held but as a pawn
	To wage against thine enemies; ne'er feared to lose it,
	Thy safety being motive.
LEAR	Out of my sight!
KENT	See better, Lear, and let me still remain
	The true blank of thine eye.
LEAR	Now by Apollo –
KENT	Now by Apollo, King,
	Thou swear'st thy gods in vain.
LEAR	O vassal! miscreant! 160

[*He draws his sword.*

ALBANY, CORNWALL	Dear sir, forbear!
KENT	Kill thy physician, and the fee bestow
	Upon the foul disease. Revoke thy gift,
	Or, whilst I can vent clamour from my throat,
	I'll tell thee thou dost evil.
LEAR	Hear me, recreant;
	On thine allegiance, hear me!
	That thou hast sought to make us break our vows –
	Which we durst never yet – and with strained pride
	To come betwixt our sentence and our power –

Which nor our nature nor our place can bear, –   170
Our potency made good, take thy reward.
Five days we do allot thee for provision
To shield thee from disasters of the world,
And on the sixth to turn thy hated back
Upon our kingdom. If, on the tenth day following,
Thy banished trunk be found in our dominions,
The moment is thy death. Away! By Jupiter,
This shall not be revoked.

KENT   Fare thee well, King; sith thus thou wilt appear,
Freedom lives hence, and banishment is here.   180
[*To Cordelia:*]
The gods to their dear shelter take thee, maid,
That justly think'st and hast most rightly said;
[*to Goneril and Regan:*]
And your large speeches may your deeds approve,
That good effects may spring from words of love. –
Thus Kent, O princes, bids you all adieu;
He'll shape his old course in a country new.   [*Exit.*

> *Flourish. Enter* GLOUCESTER *with* FRANCE,
> BURGUNDY *and* ATTENDANTS.

GLO'STER   Here's France and Burgundy, my noble lord.
LEAR   My lord of Burgundy,
We first address toward you, who with this king
Hath rivalled for our daughter. What in the least   190
Will you require in present dower with her,
Or cease your quest of love?
BURGUNDY   Most royal Majesty,
I crave no more than hath your Highness offered –
Nor will you tender less?
LEAR   Right noble Burgundy,
When she was dear to us, we did hold her so;
But now her price is fall'n. Sir, there she stands.
If aught within that little-seeming substance,
Or all of it, with our displeasure pieced,
And nothing more, may fitly like your Grace,
She's there, and she is yours.
BURGUNDY   I know no answer.   200
LEAR   Will you, with those infirmities she owes,

Unfriended, new adopted to our hate,
Dow'red with our curse and strangered with our oath,
Take her or leave her?
BURGUNDY   Pardon me, royal sir.
Election makes not up on such conditions.[9]
LEAR   Then leave her, sir; for, by the power that made me,
I tell you all her wealth. [*To France:*] For you, great king,
I would not from your love make such a stray
To match you where I hate; therefore beseech you
T'avert your liking a more worthier way   210
Than on a wretch whom Nature is ashamed
Almost t'acknowledge hers.
FRANCE   This is most strange,
That she whom even but now was your best object,
The argument of your praise, balm of your age,
The best, the dearest, should in this trice of time
Commit a thing so monstrous, to dismantle
So many folds of favour. Sure her offence
Must be of such unnatural degree
That monsters it, or your fore-vouched affection
Fall into taint; which to believe of her   220
Must be a faith that reason without miracle
Should never plant in me.
CORDELIA   I yet beseech your Majesty –
If for I want that glib and oily art
To speak and purpose not, since what I well intend,
I'll do't before I speak – that you make known
It is no vicious blot, murder, or foulness,
No unchaste action or dishonoured step,
That hath deprived me of your grace and favour;
But even for want of that for which I am richer –
A still-soliciting eye, and such a tongue   230
That I am glad I have not, though not to have it
Hath lost me in your liking.
LEAR   Better thou
Hadst not been born, than not t'have pleased me better.
FRANCE   Is it but this – a tardiness in nature,
Which often leaves the history unspoke
That it intends to do? My lord of Burgundy,

What say you to the lady? Love's not love
When it is mingled with regards that stands
Aloof from th'entire point.[10] Will you have her?
She is herself a dowry.

BURGUNDY   Royal King,   240
Give but that portion which yourself proposed,
And here I take Cordelia by the hand,
Duchess of Burgundy.

LEAR   Nothing. I have sworn; I am firm.

BURGUNDY [to Cordelia:] I am sorry then you have so lost a father
That you must lose a husband.

CORDELIA   Peace be with Burgundy.
Since that respect and fortunes are his love,
I shall not be his wife.

FRANCE   Fairest Cordelia, that art most rich, being poor;
Most choice, forsaken; and most loved, despised;   250
Thee and thy virtues here I seize upon.
Be it lawful I take up what's cast away.
Gods, gods! 'Tis strange that from their cold'st neglect.
My love should kindle to inflamed respect.
Thy dow'rless daughter, King, thrown to my chance,
Is Queen of us, of ours, and our fair France.
Not all the dukes of wat'rish Burgundy
Can buy this unprized precious maid of me.
Bid them farewell, Cordelia, though unkind;
Thou losest here, a better where to find.   260

LEAR   Thou hast her, France; let her be thine, for we
Have no such daughter, nor shall ever see
That face of hers again. Therefore be gone
Without our grace, our love, our benison.
Come, noble Burgundy.

Flourish. Exeunt LEAR, BURGUNDY, CORNWALL, ALBANY,
          GLOUCESTER, EDMUND *and* ATTENDANTS.

FRANCE   Bid farewell to your sisters.

CORDELIA The jewels of our father, with washed eyes
Cordelia leaves you. I know you what you are,
And like a sister am most loath to call
Your faults as they are named. Love well our father:
To your professèd bosoms I commit him;   270

But yet, alas, stood I within his grace,
I would prefer him to a better place.
So farewell to you both.

REGAN   Prescribe not us our duty.

GONERIL   Let your study
Be to content your lord, who hath received you
At Fortune's alms. You have obedience scanted,
And well are worth the want that you have wanted.[11]

CORDELIA   Time shall unfold what plighted cunning hides,
Who covert faults at last with shame derides.[12]
Well may you prosper.

FRANCE   Come, my fair Cordelia.   280
                    [*Exeunt France and Cordelia.*

GONERIL   Sister, it is not little I have to say of what most nearly
appertains to us both. I think our father will hence
tonight.

REGAN   That's most certain, and with you; next month with us.

GONERIL   You see how full of changes his age is. The observa-
tion we have made of it hath not been little. He always
loved our sister most, and with what poor judgement
he hath now cast her off appears too grossly.

REGAN   'Tis the infirmity of his age; yet he hath ever but
slenderly known himself.   290

GONERIL   The best and soundest of his time hath been but rash;[13]
then must we look from his age to receive, not alone
the imperfections of long-ingraffed condition, but
therewithal the unruly waywardness that infirm and
choleric years bring with them.

REGAN   Such unconstant starts are we like to have from him as
this of Kent's banishment.

GONERIL   There is further compliment of leave-taking between
France and him. Pray you let us hit together. If our
father carry authority with such disposition as he   300
bears,[14] this last surrender of his will but offend us.

REGAN   We shall further think of it.

GONERIL   We must do something, and i'th'heat.
                                      [*Exeunt.*

SCENE 2.

A room in the Earl of Gloucester's house.

Enter EDMUND, *holding a letter.*

EDMUND   Thou, Nature, art my goddess;[15] to thy law
My services are bound. Wherefore should I
Stand in the plague of custom,[16] and permit
The curiosity of nations to deprive me,
For that I am some twelve or fourteen moonshines
Lag of a brother? Why bastard? Wherefore base?
When my dimensions are as well compáct,
My mind as generous, and my shape as true,
As honest madam's issue? Why brand they us
With 'base', with 'baseness', 'bastardy', 'base, base',   10
Who, in the lusty stealth of nature, take
More composition and fierce quality
Than doth, within a dull, stale, tired bed,
Go to th'creating a whole tribe of fops
Got 'tween a sleep and wake? Well then,
Legitimate Edgar, I must have your land.
Our father's love is to the bastard Edmund
As to th'legitimate. Fine word, 'legitimate'!
Well, my legitimate, if this letter speed,
And my invention thrive, Edmund the base   20
Shall top th'legitimate.[17] I grow, I prosper.
Now, gods, stand up for bastards!

Enter GLOUCESTER.

GLO'STER   Kent banished thus? And France in choler parted?
And the King gone tonight? Prescribed his power,
Confined to exhibition? All this done
Upon the gad? – Edmund, how now? What news?

EDMUND   So please your lordship, none.
                        [*He hastily puts the letter into his pocket.*

GLO'STER   Why so earnestly seek you to put up that letter?

EDMUND   I know no news, my lord.

GLO'STER   What paper were you reading?   30

EDMUND   Nothing, my lord.

GLO'STER   No? What needed then that terrible dispatch of it into
           your pocket? The quality of 'nothing' hath not such
           need to hide itself. Let's see. Come, if it be nothing, I
           shall not need spectacles.

EDMUND   I beseech you, sir, pardon me. It is a letter from my
           brother that I have not all o'er-read; and for so much as
           I have perused, I find it not fit for your o'er-looking.

GLO'STER   Give me the letter, sir.

EDMUND   I shall offend either to detain or give it: the contents,   40
           as in part I understand them, are to blame.

GLO'STER   Let's see, let's see.   [*Edmund gives him the letter.*

EDMUND   I hope, for my brother's justification, he wrote this but
           as an essay or taste of my virtue.

GLO'STER   [*reads:*] 'This policy and reverence of age makes the
           world bitter to the best of our times, keeps our fortunes
           from us till our oldness cannot relish them. I begin to
           find an idle and fond bondage in the oppression of aged
           tyranny, who sways, not as it hath power, but as it is
           suffered. Come to me, that of this I may speak more. If   50
           our father would sleep till I waked him, you should
           enjoy half his revenue for ever, and live the beloved of
           your brother. Edgar.'
               Hum! Conspiracy? 'Sleep till I waked him, you
           should enjoy half his revenue'. My son Edgar: had he a
           hand to write this? A heart and brain to breed it in?
           When came you to this? Who brought it?

EDMUND   It was not brought me, my lord: there's the cunning of
           it. I found it thrown in at the casement of my closet.

GLO'STER   You know the character to be your brother's?   60

EDMUND   If the matter were good, my lord, I durst swear it were
           his; but, in respect of that, I would fain think it were not.

GLO'STER   It is his.

EDMUND   It is his hand, my lord; but I hope his heart is not in
           the contents.

GLO'STER   Has he never before sounded you in this business?

EDMUND   Never, my lord. But I have heard him oft maintain it
           to be fit that, sons at perfect age, and fathers declined,
           the father should be as ward to the son, and the son
           manage his revenue.   70

GLO'STER   O villain, villain: his very opinion in the letter! Abhorred villain! Unnatural, detested, brutish villain; worse than brutish! Go, sirrah, seek him: I'll apprehend him. Abominable villain! Where is he?

EDMUND   I do not well know, my lord. If it shall please you to suspend your indignation against my brother till you can derive from him better testimony of his intent, you should run a certain course; where, if you violently proceed against hum, mistaking his purpose, it would make a great gap in your own honour, and shake in 80 pieces the heart of his obedience. I dare pawn down my life for him that he hath writ this to feel my affection to your honour, and to no other pretence of danger.

GLO'STER   Think you so?

EDMUND   If your honour judge it meet, I will place you where you shall hear us confer of this, and by an auricular assurance have your satisfaction, and that without any further delay than this very evening.

GLO'STER   He cannot be such a monster –   90

EDMUND   Nor is not, sure –

GLO'STER   To his father, that so tenderly and entirely loves him. Heaven and earth![18] Edmund, seek him out; wind me into him, I pray you: frame the business after your own wisdom. I would unstate myself, to be in a due resolution.[19]

EDMUND   I will seek him, sir, presently, convey the business as I shall find means, and acquaint you withal.

GLO'STER   These late eclipses in the sun and moon portend no good to us. Though the wisdom of nature can reason 100 it thus and thus, yet nature finds itself scourged by the sequent effects. Love cools, friendship falls off, brothers divide. In cities, mutinies; in countries, discord; in palaces, treason; and the bond cracked 'twixt son and father. This villain of mine comes under the prediction: there's son against father; the King falls from bias of nature: there's father against child. We have seen the best of our time. Machinations, hollowness, treachery and all ruinous disorders follow us disquietly

to our graves.[20] Find out this villain, Edmund; it shall 110
lose thee nothing; do it carefully. And the noble and
true-hearted Kent banished; his offence, honesty! 'Tis
strange.   [*Exit.*

EDMUND   This is the excellent foppery of the world, that when
we are sick in fortune, often the surfeits of our own
behaviour, we make guilty of our disasters the sun, the
moon and stars; as if we were villains on necessity, fools
by heavenly compulsion, knaves, thieves and treachers
by spherical predominance, drunkards, liars and
adulterers by an enforced obedience of planetary 120
influence, and all that we are evil in by a divine
thrusting on. An admirable evasion of whoremaster
man, to lay his goatish disposition on the charge of a
star! My father compounded with my mother under the
Dragon's tail, and my nativity was under Ursa Major, so
that it follows I am rough and lecherous. Fut![21] I should
have been that I am, had the maidenliest star in the
firmament twinkled on my bastardizing. Edgar –

Enter EDGAR.

Pat: he comes like the catastrophe of the old comedy.[22]
My cue is villainous melancholy, with a sigh like 130
Tom o'Bedlam.[23] – O, these eclipses do portend these
divisions. Fa, sol, la, me.[24]

EDGAR   How now, brother Edmund? What serious contem-
plation are you in?

EDMUND   I am thinking, brother, of a prediction I read this other
day, what should follow these eclipses.

EDGAR   Do you busy yourself with that?

EDMUND   I promise you, the effects he writes of succeed unhappily, as of unnaturalness between the child and the
parent, death, dearth, dissolutions of ancient amities, 140
divisions in state, menaces and maledictions against
king and nobles, needless diffidences, banishment of
friends, dissipation of cohorts, nuptial breaches, and I
know not what.

EDGAR   How long have you been a sectary astronomical?[25]

EDMUND   When saw you my father last?

EDGAR   The night gone by.

EDMUND   Spake you with him?

EDGAR   Ay, two hours together.

EDMUND   Parted you in good terms? Found you no displeasure 150
           in him, by word nor countenance?

EDGAR   None at all.

EDMUND   Bethink yourself wherein you may have offended him;
           and at my entreaty forbear his presence until some
           little time hath qualified the heat of his displeasure,
           which at this instant so rageth in him that with the
           mischief of your person it would scarcely allay.

EDGAR   Some villain hath done me wrong.

EDMUND   That's my fear. I pray you have a continent forbear-
           ance till the speed of his rage goes slower; and, as I say, 160
           retire with me to my lodging, from whence I will fitly
           bring you to hear my lord speak. Pray ye, go; there's
           my key. If you do stir abroad, go armed.

EDGAR   Armed, brother?[26]

EDMUND   Brother, I advise you to the best. I am no honest man
           if there be any good meaning toward you. I have told
           you what I have seen and heard – but faintly, nothing
           like the image and horror of it. Pray you, away!

EDGAR   Shall I hear from you anon?

EDMUND   I do serve you in this business.   [Exit Edgar. 170
           A credulous father; and a brother noble,
           Whose nature is so far from doing harms
           That he suspects none – on whose foolish honesty
           My practices ride easy. I see the business.
           Let me, if not by birth, have lands by wit:
           All with me's meet that I can fashion fit.   [Exit.

SCENE 3.

A room in the Duke of Albany's house.

Enter GONERIL *and* OSWALD, *her steward.*

GONERIL Did my father strike my gentleman for chiding of his
Fool?

OSWALD Ay, madam.

GONERIL By day and night he wrongs me. Every hour
He flashes into one gross crime or other
That sets us all at odds. I'll not endure it.
His knights grow riotous, and himself upbraids us
On every trifle. When he returns from hunting,
I will not speak with him: say I am sick.
If you come slack of former services,   10
You shall do well; the fault of it I'll answer.

[*Horns heard.*

OSWALD He's coming, madam; I hear him.

GONERIL Put on what weary negligence you please,
You and your fellows; I'd have it come to question.
If he distaste it, let him to my sister,
Whose mind and mine I know in that are one,
Not to be overruled. Idle old man,
That still would manage those authorities
That he hath given away! Now, by my life,
Old fools are babes again, and must be used   20
With checks as flatteries, when they are seen abused.[27]
Remember what I have said.

OSWALD   Very well, madam.

GONERIL And let his knights have colder looks among you;
What grows of it, no matter. Advise your fellows so.
I would breed from hence occasions, and I shall,
That I may speak.[28] I'll write straight to my sister
To hold my very course. Prepare for dinner.

[*Exeunt.*

SCENE 4.

A hall in Albany's house.

Enter KENT, *disguised as 'Caius'.*

KENT   If but as well I other accents borrow,
That can my speech diffuse, my good intent
May carry through itself to that full issue
For which I razed my likeness. Now, banished Kent,
If thou canst serve where thou dost stand condemned,
So may it come thy master whom thou lov'st
Shall find thee full of labours.

Horns heard. Enter LEAR, *with* KNIGHTS *and* ATTENDANTS.[29]

LEAR   Let me not stay a jot for dinner; go, get it ready.
                                                    [*Exit attendant.*
How now? What art thou?

KENT   A man, sir.   10

LEAR   What dost thou profess? What would'st thou with us?

KENT   I do profess to be no less than I seem, to serve him
truly that will put me in trust, to love him that is
honest, to converse with him that is wise and says
little, to fear judgement, to fight when I cannot
choose, and to eat no fish.[30]

LEAR   What art thou?

KENT   A very honest-hearted fellow, and as poor as the King.

LEAR   If thou be'st as poor for a subject as he's for a king,
thou art poor enough. What would'st thou?   20

KENT   Service.

LEAR   Who would'st thou serve?

KENT   You.

LEAR   Dost thou know me, fellow?

KENT   No, sir; but you have that in your countenance which
I would fain call master.

LEAR   What's that?

KENT   Authority.

LEAR   What services canst thou do?

KENT   I can keep honest counsel, ride, run, mar a curious tale   30
in telling it, and deliver a plain message bluntly; that

which ordinary men are fit for, I am qualified in; and the best of me is diligence.

LEAR   How old art thou?

KENT   Not so young, sir, to love a woman for singing, nor so old to dote on her for anything. I have years on my back forty-eight.

LEAR   Follow me; thou shalt serve me. If I like thee no worse after dinner, I will not part from thee yet. – Dinner, ho! Dinner! Where's my knave? My Fool? Go you and 40 call my Fool hither.   [*Exit attendant.*

Enter OSWALD.

You, you, sirrah! Where's my daughter?

OSWALD   [*crossing the hall without pausing:*] So please you –
                                        [*Exit.*

LEAR   What says the fellow there? Call the clotpoll back!
                                    [*Exit a knight.*

Where's my Fool? Ho! I think the world's asleep.

Enter the KNIGHT.

How now? Where's that mongrel?

KNIGHT   He says, my lord, your daughter is not well.

LEAR   Why came not the slave back to me when I called him?

KNIGHT   Sir, he answered me in the roundest manner, he would not.   50

LEAR   He would not?

KNIGHT   My lord, I know not what the matter is, but to my judgement your Highness is not entertained with that ceremonious affection as you were wont. There's a great abatement of kindness appears as well in the general dependants as in the Duke himself also and your daughter.

LEAR   Ha? Say'st thou so?

KNIGHT   I beseech you pardon me, my lord, if I be mistaken, for my duty cannot be silent when I think your Highness 60 wronged.

LEAR   Thou but rememb'rest me of mine own conception. I have perceived a most faint neglect of late, which I have rather blamed as mine own jealous curiosity than as a very pretence and purpose of unkindness; I will

	look further into't. But where's my Fool? I have not seen him this two days.
KNIGHT	Since my young lady's going into France, sir, the Fool hath much pined away.
LEAR	No more of that; I have noted it well. Go you and tell 70 my daughter I would speak with her. [*Exit attendant.*
	Go you, call hither my Fool. [*Exit another attendant.*

Enter OSWALD.

	O you sir, you, come you hither, sir. Who am I, sir?
OSWALD	My lady's father.
LEAR	'My lady's father', my lord's knave? You whoreson dog, you slave, you cur!
OSWALD	I am none of these, my lord; I beseech your pardon.
LEAR	Do you bandy looks with me, you rascal? [*He strikes him.*
OSWALD	I'll not be strucken, my lord.
KENT	Nor tripped neither, you base football player.³¹ 80
	[*Kent trips Oswald, who falls.*
LEAR	I thank thee, fellow. Thou serv'st me, and I'll love thee.
KENT	[*to Oswald:*] Come, sir, arise, away! I'll teach you differences. Away, away! If you will measure your lubber's length again, tarry; but away! Go to; have you wisdom? So. [*Exit Oswald.*
LEAR	Now, my friendly knave, I thank thee. There's earnest of thy service. [*He gives money to Kent.*]

Enter FOOL.

FOOL	Let me hire him too: here's my coxcomb.
	[*He offers Kent his cap.*
LEAR	How now, my pretty knave? How dost thou?
FOOL	[*to Kent:*] Sirrah, you were best take my coxcomb. 90
KENT	Why, Fool?
FOOL	Why? For taking one's part that's out of favour. Nay, an thou canst not smile as the wind sits, thou'lt catch cold shortly.³² There, take my coxcomb. Why, this fellow has banished two on's daughters, and did the third a blessing against his will. If thou follow him, thou must needs wear my coxcomb. – How now, nuncle? Would I had two coxcombs and two daughters!
LEAR	Why, my boy?

FOOL	If I gave them all my living, I'd keep my coxcombs my- 100 self. There's mine; beg another of thy daughters.
LEAR	Take heed, sirrah – the whip.
FOOL	Truth's a dog that must to kennel; he must be whipped out, when the Lady Brach may stand by th'fire and stink.
LEAR	A pestilent gall to me.
FOOL	Sirrah, I'll teach thee a speech.
LEAR	Do.
FOOL	Mark it, nuncle:

> Have more than thou showest,
> Speak less than thou knowest, 110
> Lend less than thou owest,
> Ride more than thou goest,
> Learn more than thou trowest,
> Set less than thou throwest;
> Leave thy drink and thy whore,
> And keep in-a-door,
> And thou shalt have more
> Than two tens to a score.[33]

KENT	This is nothing, Fool.
FOOL	Then 'tis like the breath of an unfee'd lawyer – you gave 120 me nothing for't. Can you make no use of nothing, nuncle?
LEAR	Why, no, boy: nothing can be made out of nothing.
FOOL	[to Kent:] Prithee tell him, so much the rent of his land comes to. He will not believe a Fool.
LEAR	A bitter Fool.
FOOL	Dost thou know the difference, my boy, between a bitter Fool and a sweet one?
LEAR	No, lad; teach me.
FOOL	That lord that counselled thee 130

> To give away thy land,
> Come place him here by me;
> Do thou for him stand.
> The sweet and bitter Fool
> Will presently appear:
> The one in motley here,   [He points to himself.
> The other found out there!   [He points to Lear.

LEAR	Dost thou call me fool, boy?

FOOL   All thy other titles thou hast given away; that, thou
          wast born with.   140
KENT   This is not altogether fool, my lord.
FOOL   No, faith, lords and great men will not let me: if I had
          a monopoly out, they would have part on't; and ladies
          too, they will not let me have all the fool to myself;
          they'll be snatching.³⁴ Nuncle, give me an egg, and I'll
          give thee two crowns.
LEAR   What two crowns shall they be?
FOOL   Why, after I have cut the egg i'th'middle and eat up the
          meat, the two crowns of the egg. When thou clovest
          thy crown i'th'middle and gav'st away both parts, thou   150
          bor'st thine ass on thy back o'er the dirt. Thou hadst
          little wit in thy bald crown when thou gav'st thy golden
          one away. If I speak like myself in this, let him be
          whipped that first finds it so.
          [*He sings:*]
                    Fools had ne'er less grace in a year;
                        For wise men are grown foppish,
                    And know not how their wits to wear,
                        Their manners are so apish.³⁵
LEAR   When were you wont to be so full of songs, sirrah?
FOOL   I have used it, nuncle, e'er since thou mad'st thy   160
          daughters thy mothers; for when thou gav'st them the
          rod and putt'st down thine own breeches,
          [*He sings:*]
                    Then they for sudden joy did weep,
                        And I for sorrow sung,
                    That such a king should play bo-peep,
                        And go the fools among.
          Prithee, nuncle, keep a schoolmaster that can teach thy
          Fool to lie: I would fain learn to lie.
LEAR   An you lie, sirrah, we'll have you whipped.
FOOL   I marvel what kin thou and thy daughters are: they'll   170
          have me whipped for speaking true, thou'lt have me
          whipped for lying; and sometimes I am whipped for
          holding my peace. I had rather be any kind o' thing
          than a Fool, and yet I would not be thee, nuncle: thou
          hast pared thy wit o'both sides and left nothing i'th'

middle. Here comes one o'the parings.

Enter GONERIL.

LEAR   How now, daughter? What makes that frontlet on?
Methinks you are too much of late i'th'frown.

FOOL   Thou wast a pretty fellow when thou hadst no need to
care for her frowning; now thou art an O without a 180
figure.[36] I am better than thou art now: I am a Fool, thou
art nothing. [*To Goneril:*] Yes, forsooth, I will hold my
tongue; so your face bids me, though you say nothing.
    Mum, mum.
    He that keeps nor crust nor crumb,
    Weary of all, shall want some.[37]
[*He points to Lear:*] That's a shealed peascod.

GONERIL Not only, sir, this your all-licensed Fool
But other of your insolent retinue
Do hourly carp and quarrel, breaking forth   190
In rank and not-to-be-endured riots. Sir,
I had thought, by making this well known unto you,
To have found a safe redress; but now grow fearful,
By what yourself too late have spoke and done,
That you protect this course, and put it on
By your allowance; which if you should, the fault
Would not scape censure, nor the redresses sleep
Which, in the tender of a wholesome weal,
Might in their working do you that offence
Which else were shame, that then necessity   200
Will call discreet proceeding.[38]

FOOL   For you know, nuncle,
    The hedge-sparrow fed the cuckoo so long
    That it had it head bit off by it young.
So out went the candle, and we were left darkling.

LEAR   Are you our daughter?

GONERIL I would you would make use of your good wisdom
(Whereof I know you are fraught) and put away
These dispositions which of late transport you
From what you rightly are.   210

FOOL   May not an ass know when the cart draws the horse?
[*He sings:*] Whoop, Jug! I love thee.[39]

LEAR   Does any here know me? This is not Lear.
            Does Lear walk thus, speak thus? Where are his eyes?
            Either his notion weakens, or his discernings
            Are lethargied. Ha! Waking? 'Tis not so?
            Who is it that can tell me who I am?
FOOL   Lear's shadow.
LEAR   I would learn that; for by the marks
            Of sovereignty, knowledge, and reason,
            I should be false persuaded I had daughters.   220
FOOL   Which they will make an obedient father.[40]
LEAR   Your name, fair gentlewoman?
GONERIL   This admiration, sir, is much o'th'savour
            Of other your new pranks.[41] I do beseech you
            To understand my purposes aright:
            As you are old and reverend, should be wise.
            Here do you keep a hundred knights and squires,
            Men so disordered, so debauched and bold,
            That this our court, infected with their manners,
            Shows like a riotous inn. Epicurism and lust   230
            Makes it more like a tavern or a brothel
            Than a graced palace. The shame itself doth speak
            For instant remedy. Be then desired,
            By her that else will take the thing she begs,
            A little to disquantity your train;
            And the remainders, that shall still depend,
            To be such men as may besort your age,
            Which know themselves and you.
LEAR   Darkness and devils!
            Saddle my horses; call my train together!
            Degenerate bastard, I'll not trouble thee;   240
            Yet have I left a daughter.
GONERIL   You strike my people, and your disordered rabble
            Make servants of their betters.

                            Enter ALBANY.

LEAR   Woe that too late repents! – O, are you come?
            Is it your will? Speak, sir! – Prepare my horses. –
            Ingratitude, thou marble-hearted fiend,
            More hideous when thou show'st thee in a child
            Than the sea-monster!

ALBANY	Pray, sir, be patient.
LEAR	[*To Goneril:*] Detested kite, thou liest!

My train are men of choice and rarest parts,   250
That all particulars of duty know,
And in the most exact regard support
The worships of their name. − O most small fault,[42]
How ugly didst thou in Cordelia show,
Which, like an engine, wrenched my frame of nature
From the fixed place,[43] drew from my heart all love,
And added to the gall. O Lear, Lear, Lear!
[*He strikes his head:*] Beat at this gate that let thy folly in
And thy dear judgement out! − Go, go, my people.
                 [*Exeunt knights, attendants and Kent.*

ALBANY   My lord, I am guiltless as I am ignorant   260
Of what hath moved you.

LEAR   It may be so, my lord. −
Hear, Nature; hear, dear goddess; hear!
Suspend thy purpose, if thou didst intend
To make this creature fruitful.
Into her womb convey sterility,
Dry up in her the organs of increase,
And from her derogate body never spring
A babe to honour her. If she must teem,
Create her child of spleen, that it may live
And be a thwart disnatured torment to her.   270
Let it stamp wrinkles in her brow of youth,
With cadent tears fret channels in her cheeks,
Turn all her mother's pains and benefits
To laughter and contempt, that she may feel
How sharper than a serpent's tooth it is
To have a thankless child!   Away, away!   [*Exit Lear.*

ALBANY   Now, gods that we adore, whereof comes this?
GONERIL   Never afflict yourself to know more of it,
But let his disposition have that scope
As dotage gives it.   280

                 Enter LEAR.

LEAR   What, fifty of my followers at a clap?
Within a fortnight?

ALBANY   What's the matter, sir?

LEAR   I'll tell thee. [*To Goneril:*] Life and death! I am ashamed
            That thou hast power to shake my manhood thus;
            That these hot tears, which break from me perforce,
            Should make thee worth them. Blasts and fogs upon
                                                            thee!
            Th'untented woundings of a father's curse
            Pierce every sense about thee! Old fond eyes,
            Beweep this cause again, I'll pluck ye out,
            And cast you, with the waters that you loose,   290
            To temper clay. Yea, is't come to this?
            Ha! Let it be so. I have another daughter,
            Who I am sure is kind and comfortable.
            When she shall hear this of thee, with her nails
            She'll flay thy wolvish visage. Thou shalt find
            That I'll resume the shape which thou dost think
            I have cast off for ever.   [*Exit.*

GONERIL   Do you mark that?

ALBANY   I cannot be so partial, Goneril,
            To the great love I bear you –

GONERIL   Pray you, content.
            Come, sir, no more. – What, Oswald, ho!   300
            [*To the Fool:*]
            You sir, more knave than fool, after your master!

FOOL   Nuncle Lear, nuncle Lear! Tarry; take the Fool with
            thee.
                A fox, when one has caught her,
                And such a daughter,
                Should sure to the slaughter,
                If my cap would buy a halter.
                So the Fool follows after.   [*Exit.*

GONERIL   This man hath had good counsel! A hundred knights?
            'Tis politic and safe to let him keep   310
            At point a hundred knights; yes, that on every dream,
            Each buzz, each fancy, each complaint, dislike,
            He may enguard his dotage with their powers,
            And hold our lives in mercy. Oswald, I say!

ALBANY   Well, you may fear too far.

GONERIL   Safer than trust too far.
            Let me still take away the harms I fear,

Not fear still to be taken. I know his heart.
What he hath uttered I have writ my sister.
If she sustain him and his hundred knights,
When I have showed th'unfitness — [44]   320

Enter OSWALD.

                                            How now, Oswald?
What, have you writ that letter to my sister?

OSWALD   Ay, madam.

GONERIL   Take you some company, and away to horse.
Inform her full of my particular fear,
And thereto add such reasons of your own
As may compact it more. Get you gone,
And hasten your return.   [*Exit Oswald.*
                                 No, no, my lord,
This milky gentleness and course of yours
Though I condemn not, yet, under pardon,
You are much more attasked for want of wisdom   330
Than praised for harmful mildness.

ALBANY   How far your eyes may pierce I cannot tell;
Striving to better, oft we mar what's well.

GONERIL   Nay, then —

ALBANY   Well, well; th'event.   [*Exeunt.*

SCENE 5.

Outside Albany'a house.

Enter LEAR, KENT *and* FOOL.

LEAR   Go you before to Gloucester with these letters. Ac-
          quaint my daughter no further with anything you know
          than comes from her demand out of the letter. If your
          diligence be not speedy, I shall be there afore you.

KENT   I will not sleep, my lord, till I have delivered your
          letter.   [*Exit.*

FOOL   If a man's brains were in's heels, were't not in danger
          of kibes?

LEAR   Ay, boy.

FOOL   Then I prithee be merry; thy wit shall not go slipshod. 10

LEAR	Ha, ha, ha![45]
FOOL	Shalt see thy other daughter will use thee kindly; for, though she's as like this as a crab's like an apple, yet I can tell what I can tell.
LEAR	What canst tell, boy?
FOOL	She will taste as like this as a crab does to a crab. Thou canst tell why one's nose stands i'th'middle on's face?
LEAR	No.
FOOL	Why, to keep one's eyes of either side's nose, that what a man cannot smell out, he may spy into. 20
LEAR	I did her wrong.
FOOL	Canst tell how an oyster makes his shell?
LEAR	No.
FOOL	Nor I neither; but I can tell why a snail has a house.
LEAR	Why?
FOOL	Why, to put's head in; not to give it away to his daughters, and leave his horns without a case.
LEAR	I will forget my nature. So kind a father! Be my horses ready?
FOOL	Thy asses are gone about 'em. The reason why the 30 Seven Stars are no moe than seven is a pretty reason.
LEAR	Because they are not eight.
FOOL	Yes, indeed; thou would'st make a good Fool.
LEAR	To take't again perforce! Monster Ingratitude!
FOOL	If thou wert my Fool, nuncle, I'd have thee beaten for being old before thy time.
LEAR	How's that?
FOOL	Thou should'st not have been old till thou hadst been wise.
LEAR	O let me not be mad, not mad, sweet heaven! 40 Keep me in temper; I would not be mad!

Enter a GENTLEMAN.

	How now! Are the horses ready?
GENT.	Ready, my lord.
LEAR	Come, boy.
FOOL	She that's a maid now, and laughs at my departure, Shall not be a maid long, unless things be cut shorter.[46]

[Exeunt.

ACT 2, SCENE 1.

Within the house of the Earl of Gloucester.

Enter EDMUND *and* CURAN, *meeting.*

EDMUND   Save thee, Curan.

CURAN   And you, sir. I have been with your father, and given him notice that the Duke of Cornwall and Regan his Duchess will be here with him this night.

EDMUND   How comes that?

CURAN   Nay, I know not. You have heard of the news abroad? I mean the whispered ones, for they are yet but ear-kissing arguments.

EDMUND   Not I. Pray you, what are they?

CURAN   Have you heard of no likely wars toward, 'twixt the   10
Dukes of Cornwall and Albany?

EDMUND   Not a word.

CURAN   You may do, then, in time. Fare you well, sir.   [*Exit.*

EDMUND   The Duke be here tonight? The better! Best!
This weaves itself perforce into my business.
My father hath set guard to take my brother;
And I have one thing, of a queasy question,
Which I must act. Briefness and fortune, work! –
Brother, a word! Descend, brother, I say!

Enter EDGAR.

My father watches: O sir, fly this place!   20
Intelligence is given where you are hid.
You have now the good advantage of the night.
Have you not spoken 'gainst the Duke of Cornwall?
He's coming hither, now i'th'night, i'th'haste,
And Regan with him. Have you nothing said
Upon his party 'gainst the Duke of Albany?
Advise yourself.

EDGAR   I am sure on't, not a word.

EDMUND   I hear my father coming. Pardon me:
In cunning I must draw my sword upon you.
Draw, seem to defend yourself; now quit you well. –   30

Yield! Come before my father. – Light, ho! Here! –
Fly, brother. – Torches, torches! – So farewell.

[Exit Edgar.

Some blood drawn on me would beget opinion
Of my more fierce endeavour.   *[He cuts his arm.*

I have seen drunkards
Do more than this in sport. – Father, father! –
Stop, stop! – No help?

Enter GLOUCESTER, *and* SERVANTS *with torches.*

GLO'STER   Now, Edmund, where's the villain?
EDMUND   Here stood he in the dark, his sharp sword out,
          Mumbling of wicked charms, conjuring the moon
          To stand auspicious mistress.
GLO'STER   But where is he?
EDMUND   Look, sir, I bleed.
GLO'STER   Where is the villain, Edmund?   40
EDMUND   Fled this way, sir, when by no means he could –
GLO'STER [*to servants:*] Pursue him, ho! Go after. [*Exeunt servants.*
                              'By no means' what?
EDMUND   Persuade me to the murder of your lordship;
          But that I told him the revenging gods
          'Gainst parricides did all the thunder bend,
          Spoke with how manifold and strong a bond
          The child was bound to th'father. Sir, in fine,
          Seeing how loathly opposite I stood
          To his unnatural purpose, in fell motion
          With his preparèd sword he charges home   50
          My unprovided body, latched mine arm;
          And when he saw my best alarumed spirits,
          Bold in the quarrel's right, roused to th'encounter,
          Or whether gasted by the noise I made,
          Full suddenly he fled.
GLO'STER   Let him fly far:
          Not in this land shall he remain uncaught;
          And found – dispatch! The noble Duke my master,
          My worthy arch and patron, comes tonight.
          By his authority I will proclaim it
          That he which finds him shall deserve our thanks,   60

Bringing the murderous coward to the stake;
He that conceals him, death.
EDMUND   When I dissuaded him from his intent,
And found him pight to do it, with curst speech
I threatened to discover him. He replied,
'Thou unpossessing bastard, dost thou think,
If I would stand against thee, would the reposal
Of any trust, virtue or worth in thee
Make thy words faithed? No. What I should deny
(As this I would – ay, though thou didst produce   70
My very character), I'd turn it all
To thy suggestion, plot, and damnèd practice;
And thou must make a dullard of the world,
If they not thought the profits of my death
Were very pregnant and potential spurs
To make thee seek it.'
GLO'STER   O strange and fastened villain!
Would he deny his letter, said he? I never got him.

                               [*A tucket heard.*

Hark, the Duke's trumpets! I know not why he comes.
All ports I'll bar; the villain shall not scape;
The Duke must grant me that. Besides, his picture   80
I will send far and near, that all the kingdom
May have due note of him; and of my land,
Loyal and natural boy, I'll work the means
To make thee capable.⁴⁷

     Enter CORNWALL, REGAN *and* ATTENDANTS.

CORNWALL How now, my noble friend? Since I came hither,
Which I can call but now, I have heard strange news.
REGAN   If it be true, all vengeance comes too short
Which can pursue th'offender. How dost, my lord?
GLO'STER O madam, my old heart is cracked, it's cracked.
REGAN   What, did my father's godson seek your life?   90
He whom my father named, your Edgar?
GLO'STER O lady, lady, shame would have it hid!
REGAN   Was he not companion with the riotous knights
That tended upon my father?
GLO'STER I know not, madam; 'tis too bad, too bad!

EDMUND   Yes, madam; he was of that consórt.

REGAN   No marvel, then, though he were ill affected.
           'Tis they have put him on the old man's death,
           To have th'expense and waste of his revénues.
           I have this present evening from my sister   100
           Been well informed of them, and with such cautions
           That, if they come to sojourn at my house,
           I'll not be there.

CORNWALL   Nor I, assure thee, Regan.
           Edmund, I hear that you have shown your father
           A child-like office.

EDMUND   It was my duty, sir.

GLO'STER   He did bewray his practice; and received
           This hurt you see, striving to apprehend him.

CORNWALL   Is he pursued?

GLO'STER   Ay, my good lord.

CORNWALL   If he be taken, he shall never more
           Be feared of doing harm. Make your own purpose,   110
           How in my strength you please.[48] For you, Edmund,
           Whose virtue and obedience doth this instant
           So much commend itself, you shall be ours.
           Natures of such deep trust we shall much need;
           You we first seize on.

EDMUND   I shall serve you, sir,
           Truly, however else.

GLO'STER   For him I thank your Grace.

CORNWALL   You know not why we came to visit you –

REGAN   Thus out of season, threading dark-eyed night:
           Occasions, noble Gloucester, of some prize,
           Wherein we must have use of your advice.   120
           Our father he hath writ, so hath our sister,
           Of differences, which I best thought it fit
           To answer from our home. The several messengers
           From hence attend dispatch. Our good old friend,
           Lay comforts to your bosom, and bestow
           Your needful counsel to our businesses,
           Which craves the instant use.

GLO'STER   I serve you, madam.
           Your Graces are right welcome.   [Exeunt. Flourish.

SCENE 2.

Outside Gloucester's house.

Enter KENT *and* OSWALD, *meeting.*

OSWALD   Good dawning to thee, friend. Art of this house?

KENT   Ay.

OSWALD   Where may we set our horses?

KENT   I'th'mire.

OSWALD   Prithee, if thou lov'st me, tell me.

KENT   I love thee not.

OSWALD   Why then, I care not for thee.

KENT   If I had thee in Lipsbury Pinfold,[49] I would make thee
          care for me.

OSWALD   Why dost thou use me thus? I know thee not.   10

KENT   Fellow, I know thee.

OSWALD   What dost thou know me for?

KENT   A knave, a rascal, an eater of broken meats; a base,
          proud, shallow, beggarly, three-suited, hundred-pound,
          filthy worsted-stocking knave; a lily-livered, action-
          taking, whoreson, glass-gazing, super-serviceable, finical
          rogue; one-trunk-inheriting slave; one that wouldst be a
          bawd in way of good service,[50] and art nothing but the
          composition of a knave, beggar, coward, pandar, and
          the son and heir of a mongrel bitch: one whom I will   20
          beat into clamorous whining, if thou deniest the least
          syllable of thy addition.

OSWALD   Why, what a monstrous fellow art thou, thus to rail on
          one that is neither known of thee nor knows thee!

KENT   What a brazen-faced varlet art thou, to deny thou
          knowest me! Is it two days since I tripped up thy heels
          and beat thee before the King? [*He draws hus sword.*] Draw,
          you rogue; for, though it be night, yet the moon shines.
          I'll make a sop o'th'moonshine of you, you whoreson
          cullionly barber-monger.[51] Draw!   30

OSWALD   Away! I have nothing to do with thee.

KENT   Draw, you rascal! You come with letters against the
          King, and take Vanity the puppet's part against the

royalty of her father.[52] Draw, you rogue, or I'll so carbonado your shanks! Draw, you rascal! Come your ways!

OSWALD   Help, ho! Murder! Help!

KENT   Strike, you slave! Stand, rogue! Stand, you neat slave!
Strike!   [*He beats Oswald.*

OSWALD   Help, ho! Murder, murder!

Enter EDMUND, *with his rapier drawn.*

EDMUND   How now? What's the matter? Part!   40

KENT   With you, goodman boy, if you please! Come, I'll
flesh ye; come on, young master!

Enter CORNWALL, REGAN, GLOUCESTER *and* SERVANTS.

GLO'STER Weapons? Arms? What is the matter here?

CORNWALL Keep peace, upon your lives!
He dies that strikes again. What is the matter?

REGAN   The messengers from our sister and the King.

CORNWALL What is your difference? Speak.

OSWALD   I am scarce in breath, my lord.

KENT   No marvel, you have so bestirred your valour. You
cowardly rascal, Nature disclaims in thee; a tailor made 50
thee.

CORNWALL Thou art a strange fellow; a tailor make a man?

KENT   A tailor, sir: a stone-cutter or a painter could not have
made him so ill, though they had been but two years
o'th'trade.

CORNWALL Speak yet, how grew your quarrel?

OSWALD   This ancient ruffian, sir, whose life I have spared
At suit of his grey beard –

KENT   Thou whoreson zed, thou unnecessary letter! – My
lord, if you will give me leave, I will tread this un- 60
bolted villain into mortar, and daub the wall of a jakes
with him. – Spare my grey beard, you wagtail?

CORNWALL Peace, sirrah!
You beastly knave, know you no reverence?

KENT   Yes, sir; but anger hath a privilege.

CORNWALL Why art thou angry?

KENT   That such a slave as this should wear a sword,
Who wears no honesty. Such smiling rogues as these,
Like rats, oft bite the holy cords atwain

            Which are too intrince t'unloose; smooth every passion   70
            That in the natures of their lords rebel,
            Bring oil to fire, snow to the colder moods;
            Renege, affirm, and turn their halcyon beaks
            With every gale and vary of their masters,[53]
            Knowing nought (like dogs) but following.
            [*To Oswald:*] A plague upon your epileptic visage!
            Smile you my speeches, as I were a fool?
            Goose, if I had you upon Sarum Plain,
            I'd drive ye cackling home to Camelot.[54]

CORNWALL What, art thou mad, old fellow?   80

GLO'STER   How fell you out? Say that.

KENT   No contraries hold more antipathy
            Than I and such a knave.

CORNWALL Why dost thou call him 'knave'? What is his fault?

KENT   His countenance likes me not.

CORNWALL No more perchance does mine, nor his, nor hers.

KENT   Sirs, 'tis my occupation to be plain:
            I have seen better faces in my time
            Than stands on any shoulder that I see
            Before me at this instant.

CORNWALL   This is some fellow   90
            Who, having been praised for bluntness, doth affect
            A saucy roughness, and constrains the garb
            Quite from his nature. He cannot flatter, he!
            An honest mind and plain, he must speak truth!
            An they will take it, so; if not, he's plain.
            These kind of knaves I know, which in this plainness
            Harbour more craft and more corrupter ends
            Than twenty silly-ducking óbservants
            That stretch their duties nicely.

KENT   Sir, in good faith, in síncere verity,   100
            Under th'allowance of your great aspéct,
            Whose influence, like the wreath of radiant fire
            On flick'ring Phoebus' front[55] –

CORNWALL   What mean'st by this?

KENT   To go out of my dialect, which you discommend so
            much. I know, sir, I am no flatterer. He that beguiled
            you in a plain accent was a plain knave, which for my

part I will not be, though I should win your displeasure
to entreat me to't.[56]

CORNWALL [*to Oswald:*] What was th'offence you gave him?

OSWALD   I never gave him any.   110
It pleased the King his master very late
To strike at me upon his misconstruction,
When he, compáct, and flattering his displeasure,
Tripped me behind; being down, insulted, railed,
And put upon him such a deal of man
That worthied him, got praises of the King
For him attempting who was self-subdued,
And, in the fleshment of this dread exploit,
Drew on me here again.

KENT   None of these rogues and cowards
But Ajax is their Fool.[57]

CORNWALL   Fetch forth the stocks!   120
You stubborn ancient knave, you reverend braggart,
We'll teach you!

KENT   Sir, I am too old to learn.
Call not your stocks for me; I serve the King,
On whose employment I was sent to you.
You shall do small respect, show too bold malice
Against the grace and person of my master,
Stocking his messenger.

CORNWALL   Fetch forth the stocks!
As I have life and honour, there shall he sit till noon.

REGAN   Till noon? Till night, my lord, and all night too.

KENT   Why, madam, if I were your father's dog,   130
You should not use me so.

REGAN   Sir, being his knave, I will.

CORNWALL This is a fellow of the self-same colour
Our sister speaks of. Come, bring away the stocks.

                              [*Stocks are brought out.*

GLO'STER Let me beseech your Grace not to do so.
His fault is much, and the good King, his master,
Will check him for't. Your purposed low correction
Is such as basest and contemnèd'st wretches
For pilf'rings and most common trespasses
Are punished with.[58] The King must take it ill

That he, so slightly valued in his messenger,   140
Should have him thus restrained.

CORNWALL   I'll answer that.

REGAN   My sister may receive it much more worse
To have her gentleman abused, assaulted,
For following her affairs. Put in his legs.
                              [*Kent is put in the stocks.*
Come, my good lord, away.[59]
                    [*Exeunt all except Gloucester and Kent.*

GLO'STER   I am sorry for thee, friend; 'tis the Duke's pleasure,
Whose disposition, all the world well knows,
Will not be rubbed nor stopped. I'll entreat for thee.

KENT   Pray do not, sir. I have watched, and travelled hard.
Some time I shall sleep out, the rest I'll whistle.   150
A good man's fortune may grow out at heels.
Give you good morrow!

GLO'STER   The Duke's to blame in this; 'twill be ill taken.   [*Exit.*

KENT   Good King, that must approve the common saw,
Thou out of heaven's benediction com'st
To the warm sun.[60]
Approach, thou beacon to this under globe,[61]
That by thy comfortable beams I may
Peruse this letter. Nothing almost sees miracles
But misery.[62] I know 'tis from Cordelia,   160
Who hath most fortunately been informed
Of my obscurèd course, and shall find time
From this enormous state,[63] seeking to give
Losses their remedies. All weary and o'erwatched,
Take vantage, heavy eyes, not to behold
This shameful lodging.
Fortune, good night; smile once more, turn thy wheel.[64]
                              [*He sleeps.*

SCENE 3.

Open countryside.

Enter EDGAR.

EDGAR   I heard myself proclaimed,
           And by the happy hollow of a tree
           Escaped the hunt. No port is free, no place
           That guard and most unusual vigilance
           Does not attend my taking. While I may scape,
           I will preserve myself; and am bethought
           To take the basest and most poorest shape
           That ever penury, in contempt of man,
           Brought near to beast. My face I'll grime with filth,
           Blanket my loins, elf all my hair in knots,   10
           And with presented nakedness outface
           The winds and persecutions of the sky.
           The country gives me proof and precedent
           Of Bedlam beggars[65] who, with roaring voices,
           Strike in their numbed and mortified bare arms
           Pins, wooden pricks, nails, sprigs of rosemary;
           And with this horrible object, from low farms,
           Poor pelting villages, sheepcotes and mills,
           Sometimes with lunatic bans, sometime with prayers,
           Enforce their charity. 'Poor Turlygod',[66] 'Poor Tom':   20
           That's something yet. 'Edgar', I nothing am.   [*Exit.*

SCENE 4.[67]

Outside Gloucester's house. KENT *in the stocks.*

Enter LEAR, FOOL *and* GENTLEMAN.

LEAR   'Tis strange that they should so depart from home,
           And not send back my messenger.

GENT.   As I learned,
           The night before there was no purpose in them
           Of this remove.

KENT	Hail to thee, noble master!
LEAR	Ha!

Mak'st thou this shame thy pastime?

KENT   No, my lord.

FOOL   Ha, ha! He wears cruel garters. Horses are tied by the
heads, dogs and bears by th'neck, monkeys by th'
loins, and men by th'legs. When a man's over-lusty at
legs,[68] then he wears wooden nether-stocks.   10

LEAR   What's he that hath so much thy place mistook
To set thee here?

KENT   It is both he and she,
Your son and daughter.

LEAR   No.

KENT   Yes.

LEAR   No, I say.

KENT   I say yea.

LEAR   No, no, they would not.

KENT   Yes, they have.[69]

LEAR   By Jupiter, I swear no!   20

KENT   By Juno, I swear ay!

LEAR   They durst not do't,
They could not, would not do't; 'tis worse than murder,
To do upon respect such violent outrage.
Resolve me with all modest haste which way
Thou mightst deserve or they impose this usage,
Coming from us.

KENT   My lord, when at their home
I did commend your Highness' letters to them,
Ere I was risen from the place that showed
My duty kneeling, came there a reeking post,
Stewed in his haste, half breathless, panting forth   30
From Goneril, his mistress, salutations;
Delivered letters, spite of intermission,
Which presently they read; on those conténts
They summoned up their meiny, straight took horse,
Commanded me to follow and attend
The leisure of their answer, gave me cold looks;
And meeting here the other messenger,
Whose welcome I perceived had poisoned mine –

Being the very fellow which of late
Displayed so saucily against your Highness –   40
Having more man than wit about me, drew.
He raised the house with loud and coward cries.
Your son and daughter found this trespass worth
The shame which here it suffers.

FOOL   Winter's not gone yet, if the wild geese fly that way.

    Fathers that wear rags
      Do make their children blind,
    But fathers that bear bags
      Shall see their children kind.
    Fortune, that arrant whore,   50
      Ne'er turns the key to th'poor.

But for all this thou shalt have as many dolours for thy
daughters as thou canst tell in a year.[70]

LEAR   O how this mother swells up toward my heart!
Hysterica passio![71] Down, thou climbing sorrow;
Thy element's below. Where is this daughter?

KENT   With the Earl, sir, here within.

LEAR   Follow me not; stay here.   [*Exit*.

GENT.   Made you no more offence but what you speak of?

KENT   None.   60

How chance the King comes with so small a number?

FOOL   An thou hadst been set i'th'stocks for that question,
thou'dst well deserved it.

KENT   Why, Fool?

FOOL   We'll set thee to school to an ant, to teach thee there's
no labouring i'th'winter. All that follow their noses are
led by their eyes but blind men, and there's not a nose
among twenty but can smell him that's stinking.[72] Let
go thy hold when a great wheel runs down a hill, lest it
break thy neck with following; but the great one that   70
goes upward, let him draw thee after. When a wise man
gives thee better counsel, give me mine again. I would
ha' none but knaves follow it, since a Fool gives it.

    That sir which serves and seeks for gain,
      And follows but for form,
    Will pack when it begins to rain,
      And leave thee in the storm.

	But I will tarry; the Fool will stay,
	And let the wise man fly:
	The knave turns fool that runs away;　　　　　　80
	The Fool no knave, perdy.[73]
KENT	Where learned you this, Fool?
FOOL	Not i'th'stocks, fool!

Enter LEAR *with* GLOUCESTER.

LEAR　　Deny to speak with me? 'They are sick, they are weary,
　　　　They have travelled all the night'? Mere fetches; ay,
　　　　The images of revolt and flying off.
　　　　Fetch me a better answer.

GLO'STER　　　　　　　　　　　　　My dear lord,
　　　　You know the fiery quality of the Duke,
　　　　How unremovable and fixed he is
　　　　In his own course.

LEAR　　　　　　　　　　　　Vengeance, plague, death, confusion! 90
　　　　What 'fiery quality'? Why, Gloucester, Gloucester,
　　　　I'd speak with the Duke of Cornwall and his wife.

GLO'STER　Well, my good lord, I have informed them so.

LEAR　　'Informed' them? Dost thou understand me, man?[74]

GLO'STER　Ay, my good lord.

LEAR　　The King would speak with Cornwall; the dear father
　　　　Would with his daughter speak, commands her service.[75]
　　　　Are they 'informed' of this? My breath and blood!
　　　　'Fiery'? The 'fiery' Duke? Tell the hot Duke that –
　　　　No, but not yet; may be he is not well:　　　　　　100
　　　　Infirmity doth still neglect all office
　　　　Whereto our health is bound.[76] We are not ourselves
　　　　When nature, being oppressed, commands the mind
　　　　To suffer with the body. I'll forbear,
　　　　And am fall'n out with my more headier will
　　　　To take the indisposed and sickly fit
　　　　For the sound man.[77]
　　　　[*He looks at Kent.*]　　Death on my state! Wherefore
　　　　Should he sit here? This act persuades me
　　　　That this remotion of the Duke and her
　　　　Is practice only. Give me my servant forth;　　　　110
　　　　Go tell the Duke and's wife I'd speak with them;
　　　　Now, presently: bid them come forth and hear me,

Or at their chamber door I'll beat the drum
Till it cry sleep to death.[78]

GLO'STER I would have all well betwixt you.   [*Exit.*

LEAR O me, my heart! My rising heart! But down!

FOOL Cry to it, nuncle, as the cockney did to the eels when
she put 'em i'th'paste alive. She knapped 'em o'th' cox-
combs with a stick and cried 'Down, wantons, down!'
'Twas her brother that, in pure kindness to his horse, 120
buttered his hay.[79]

Enter CORNWALL *and* REGAN, *followed by* GLOUCESTER *and* SERVANTS.

LEAR Good morrow to you both.

CORNWALL   Hail to your Grace!
                              [*Kent is set at liberty.*

REGAN I am glad to see your Highness.

LEAR Regan, I think you are. I know what reason
I have to think so; if thou shouldst not be glad,
I would divorce me from thy mother's tomb,
Sepúlchring an adultress. [*To Kent:*] O, are you free?
Some other time for that. – Belovèd Regan,
Thy sister's naught. O Regan, she hath tied
Sharp-toothed unkindness, like a vulture, here.   130
                              [*He indicates his heart.*
I can scarce speak to thee; thou'lt not believe
With how depraved a quality – O Regan!

REGAN I pray you, sir, take patience. I have hope
You less know how to value her desert
Than she to scant her duty.

LEAR   Say? How is that?

REGAN I cannot think my sister in the least
Would fail her obligation. If, sir, perchance
She have restrained the riots of your followers,
'Tis on such ground, and to such wholesome end,
As clears her from all blame.[80]   140

LEAR My curses on her!

REGAN   O sir, you are old;
Nature in you stands on the very verge
Of his confine. You should be ruled and led
By some discretion that discerns your state
Better than you yourself. Therefore I pray you

          That to our sister you do make return;
          Say you have wronged her, sir.
LEAR   Ask her forgiveness?
          Do you but mark how this becomes the house?
          [*He kneels.*] 'Dear daughter, I confess that I am old:
          Age is unnecessary; on my knees I beg   150
          That you'll vouchsafe me raiment, bed and food!'
REGAN   Good sir, no more; these are unsightly tricks.
          Return you to my sister.
LEAR   [*rising:*]   Never, Regan!
          She hath abated me of half my train,
          Looked black upon me, struck me with her tongue
          Most serpent-like upon the very heart.
          All the stored vengeances of heaven fall
          On her ingrateful top! Strike her young bones,
          You taking airs, with lameness!
CORNWALL   Fie, sir, fie!
LEAR   You nimble lightnings, dart your blinding flames   160
          Into her scornful eyes! Infect her beauty,
          You fen-sucked fogs, drawn by the pow'rful sun
          To fall and blast her pride!
REGAN   O the blest gods!
          So will you wish on me when the rash mood – [81]
LEAR   No, Regan, thou shalt never have my curse:
          Thy tender-hefted nature shall not give
          Thee o'er to harshness. Her eyes are fierce; but thine
          Do comfort and not burn. 'Tis not in thee
          To grudge my pleasures, to cut off my train,
          To bandy hasty words, to scant my sizes,   170
          And in conclusion to oppose the bolt
          Against my coming in. Thou better know'st
          The offices of nature, bond of childhood,
          Effects of courtesy, dues of gratitude;
          Thy half o'th'kingdom hast thou not forgot,
          Wherein I thee endowed.
REGAN   Good sir, to th'purpose.
LEAR   Who put my man i'th'stocks?
                             [*Tucket heard.*
CORNWALL   What trumpet's that?

REGAN   I know't: my sister's. This approves her letter,
That she would soon be here.

Enter OSWALD.

Is your lady come?
LEAR   This is a slave whose easy-borrowed pride   180
Dwells in the fickle grace of her he follows. –
Out, varlet, from my sight!
CORNWALL   What means your Grace?
LEAR   Who stocked my servant? Regan, I have good hope
Thou didst not know on't.[82]

Enter GONERIL.

Who comes here? O heavens,
If you do love old men, if your sweet sway
Allow obedience, if you yourselves are old,
Make it your cause: send down and take my part!
[*To Goneril:*] Art not ashamed to look upon this beard?
O Regan, will you take her by the hand?
GONERIL   Why not by th'hand, sir? How have I offended?   190
All's not offence that indiscretion finds
And dotage terms so.
LEAR   O sides, you are too tough!
Will you yet hold? – How came my man i'th'stocks?
CORNWALL I set him there, sir; but his own disorders
Deserved much less advancement.[83]
LEAR   You? Did you?
REGAN   I pray you, father, being weak, seem so.
If, till the expiration of your month,
You will return and sojourn with my sister,
Dismissing half your train, come then to me.
I am now from home, and out of that provision   200
Which shall be needful for your entertainment.
LEAR   Return to her? And fifty men dismissed?
No, rather I abjure all roofs, and choose
To wage against the enmity o'th'air,
To be a comrade with the wolf and owl –
Necessity's sharp pinch. Return with her?
Why, the hot-blooded France, that dowerless took
Our youngest born, I could as well be brought

To knee his throne and, squire-like, pension beg
To keep base life afoot. Return with her?   210
Persuade me rather to be slave and sumpter
To this detested groom.   [*He indicates Oswald.*

GONERIL   At your choice, sir.

LEAR   I prithee, daughter, do not make me mad.
I will not trouble thee, my child; farewell:
We'll no more meet, no more see one another.
But yet thou art my flesh, my blood, my daughter –
Or rather a disease that's in my flesh,
Which I must needs call mine. Thou art a boil,
A plague-sore, or embossèd carbuncle
In my corrupted blood. But I'll not chide thee: 220
Let shame come when it will, I do not call it;
I do not bid the thunder-bearer shoot,
Nor tell tales of thee to high-judging Jove.
Mend when thou canst; be better at thy leisure:
I can be patient; I can stay with Regan,
I and my hundred knights.

REGAN   Not altogether so.
I looked not for you yet, nor am provided
For your fit welcome. Give ear, sir, to my sister;
For those that mingle reason with your passion
Must be content to think you old, and so –   230
But she knows what she does.

LEAR   Is this well spoken?

REGAN   I dare avouch it, sir. What, fifty followers?
Is it not well? What should you need of more?
Yea, or so many, sith that both charge and danger
Speak 'gainst so great a number? How in one house
Should many people, under two commands,
Hold amity? 'Tis hard, almost impossible.

GONERIL   Why might not you, my lord, receive attendance
From those that she calls servants, or from mine?

REGAN   Why not, my lord? If then they chanced to slack ye,   240
We could control them. If you will come to me
(For now I spy a danger), I entreat you
To bring but five-and-twenty: to no more
Will I give place or notice.

LEAR   I gave you all —
REGAN   And in good time you gave it.
LEAR   Made you my guardians, my depositaries,
          But kept a reservation to be followed
          With such a number. What, must I come to you
          With five-and-twenty? Regan, said you so?
REGAN   And speak't again, my lord; no more with me.   250
LEAR   Those wicked creatures yet do look well-favoured
          When others are more wicked; not being the worst
          Stands in some rank of praise.
          [*To Goneril:*]   I'll go with thee.
          Thy fifty yet doth double five-and-twenty,
          And thou art twice her love.
GONERIL   Hear me, my lord.
          What need you five-and-twenty, ten, or five,
          To follow in a house where twice so many
          Have a command to tend you?
REGAN   What need one?
LEAR   O reason not the need! Our basest beggars
          Are in the poorest things superfluous.   260
          Allow not nature more than nature needs,
          Man's life is cheap as beast's. Thou art a lady;
          If only to go warm were gorgeous,
          Why, nature needs not what thou gorgeous wear'st,
          Which scarcely keeps thee warm. But for true need —
          You heavens, give me patience — patience I need!
          You see me here, you gods, a poor old man,
          As full of grief as age, wretched in both.
          If it be you that stirs these daughters' hearts
          Against their father, fool me not so much   270
          To bear it tamely; touch me with noble anger,
          And let not women's weapons, water-drops,
          Stain my man's cheeks. No, you unnatural hags,
          I will have such revenges on you both
          That all the world shall — I will do such things —
          What they are yet I know not, but they shall be
          The terrors of the earth! You think I'll weep;
          No, I'll not weep: [*Storm and tempest heard.*
          I have full cause of weeping, but this heart

Shall break into a hundred thousand flaws   280
Or ere I'll weep. O Fool, I shall go mad!

Exeunt LEAR, FOOL, GLOUCESTER, GENTLEMAN *and* KENT.

CORNWALL Let us withdraw; 'twill be a storm.
REGAN   This house is little: the old man and's people
          Cannot be well bestowed.
GONERIL   'Tis his own blame: hath put himself from rest,
          And must needs taste his folly.
REGAN   For his particular, I'll receive him gladly,
          But not one follower.
GONERIL   So am I purposed.
          Where is my lord of Gloucester?
CORNWALL Followed the old man forth.

Enter GLOUCESTER.

                                He is returned.   290
GLO'STER The King is in high rage.
CORNWALL   Whither is he going?
GLO'STER He calls to horse, but will I know not whither.
CORNWALL 'Tis best to give him way; he leads himself.
GONERIL   My lord, entreat him by no means to stay.
GLO'STER Alack, the night comes on, and the high winds
          Do sorely ruffle. For many miles about
          There's scarce a bush.
REGAN   O sir, to wilful men
          The injuries that they themselves procure
          Must be their schoolmasters. Shut up your doors.
          He is attended with a desperate train,   300
          And what they may incense him to, being apt
          To have his ear abused, wisdom bids fear.
CORNWALL Shut up your doors, my lord; 'tis a wild night:
          My Regan counsels well; come out o'th'storm.
                                                  [*Exeunt.*

ACT 3, SCENE 1.

A heath.

A storm with thunder and lightning.
Enter KENT *and a* GENTLEMAN, *meeting.*

KENT   Who's there, besides foul weather?

GENT.   One minded like the weather, most unquietly.

KENT   I know you. Where's the King?

GENT.   Contending with the fretful elements:
Bids the wind blow the earth into the sea,
Or swell the curlèd waters 'bove the main,
That things might change or cease; tears his white hair,
Which the impetuous blasts with eyeless rage
Catch in their fury and make nothing of;
Strives in his little world of man to out-scorn   10
The to-and-fro-conflicting wind and rain.
This night, wherein the cub-drawn bear would couch,
The lion and the belly-pinchèd wolf
Keep their fur dry, unbonneted he runs,
And bids what will take all.[84]

KENT   But who is with him?

GENT.   None but the Fool, who labours to out-jest
His heart-struck injuries.

KENT   Sir, I do know you,
And dare upon the warrant of my note
Commend a dear thing to you. There is division
(Although as yet the face of it is covered   20
With mutual cunning) 'twixt Albany and Cornwall,
Who have – as who have not that their great stars
Throned and set high? – servants, who seem no less,
Which are to France the spies and speculations
Intelligent of our state. What hath been seen,
Either in snuffs and packings of the Dukes,
Or the hard rein which both of them hath borne
Against the old kind King; or something deeper
Whereof perchance these are but furnishings – [85]
But true it is, from France there comes a power   30

Into this scattered kingdom, who already,
Wise in our negligence, have secret feet
In some of our best ports, and are at point
To show their open banner.[86] Now to you:
If on my credit you dare build so far
To make your speed to Dover, you shall find
Some that will thank you, making just report
Of how unnatural and bemadding sorrow
The King hath cause to plain.
I am a gentleman of blood and breeding,   40
And from some knowledge and assurance offer
This office to you.[87]

GENT.   I will talk further with you.

KENT   No, do not.
For confirmation that I am much more
Than my out-wall, open this purse and take
What it contains. If you shall see Cordelia
(As fear not but you shall), show her this ring,
And she will tell you who your fellow is
That yet you do not know. Fie on this storm!
I will go seek the King.   50

GENT.   Give me your hand. Have you no more to say?

KENT   Few words, but, to effect, more than all yet:
That when we have found the King (in which your pain
That way, I'll this), he that first lights on him
Holla the other.   [*Exeunt separately*.

SCENE 2.

The heath.

Storm continues. Enter LEAR *and* FOOL.

LEAR   Blow, winds, and crack your cheeks! Rage! Blow!
You cataracts and hurricanoes, spout
Till you have drenched our steeples, drowned the cocks!
You sulph'rous and thought-executing fires,
Vaunt-couriers of oak-cleaving thunderbolts,
Singe my white head! And thou, all-shaking thunder,
Strike flat the thick rotundity o'th'world,

Crack Nature's moulds, all germens spill at once
That make ingrateful man!

FOOL   O nuncle, court holy-water in a dry house is better 10
than this rain-water out o'door. Good nuncle, in; ask
thy daughters blessing. Here's a night pities neither wise
men nor fools.

LEAR   Rumble thy bellyful! Spit fire, spout rain!
Nor rain, wind, thunder, fire are my daughters.
I tax not you, you elements, with unkindness:
I never gave you kingdom, called you children;
You owe me no subscription. Then let fall
Your horrible pleasure. Here I stand your slave,
A poor, infirm, weak and despised old man;   20
But yet I call you servile ministers,
That will with two pernicious daughters join
Your high-engendered battles 'gainst a head
So old and white as this. O, ho! 'Tis foul!

FOOL   He that has a house to put's head in has a good head-
piece.
      The codpiece that will house
        Before the head has any,
      The head and he shall louse:
        So beggars marry many.   30
      The man that makes his toe
        What he his heart should make,
      Shall of a corn cry woe,
        And turn his sleep to wake.[88]
For there was never yet fair woman but she made
mouths in a glass.

Enter KENT.

LEAR   No, I will be the pattern of all patience;
I will say nothing.

KENT   Who's there?

FOOL   Marry, here's grace and a codpiece; that's a wise man 40
and a fool.

KENT   Alas, sir, are you here? Things that love night
Love not such nights as these. The wrathful skies
Gallow the very wanderers of the dark

And make them keep their caves. Since I was man,
Such sheets of fire, such bursts of horrid thunder,
Such groans of roaring wind and rain, I never
Remember to have heard. Man's nature cannot carry
Th'affliction nor the fear.

LEAR   Let the great gods,
That keep this dreadful pudder o'er our heads,   50
Find out their enemies now. Tremble, thou wretch
That hast within thee undivulgèd crimes
Unwhipped of justice. Hide thee, thou bloody hand,
Thou perjured, and thou simular of virtue
That art incestuous. Caitiff, to pieces shake,
That under covert and convenient seeming
Hast practised on man's life. Close pent-up guilts,
Rive your concealing continents, and cry
These dreadful summoners grace. I am a man
More sinned against than sinning.

KENT   Alack, bare-headed?   60
Gracious my lord, hard by here is a hovel;
Some friendship will it lend you 'gainst the tempest:
Repose you there, while I to this hard house
(More harder than the stones whereof 'tis raised,
Which even but now, demanding after you,
Denied me to come in) return, and force
Their scanted courtesy.

LEAR   My wits begin to turn. –
Come on, my boy. How dost, my boy? Art cold?
I am cold myself. – Where is this straw, my fellow?
The art of our necessities is strange,   70
And can make vild things precious. Come, your hovel.
– Poor Fool and knave, I have one part in my heart
That's sorry yet for thee.

FOOL   [sings:]
        He that has and a little tiny wit –
            With heigh-ho, the wind and the rain –
        Must make content with his fortunes fit,
            Though the rain it raineth every day.[89]

LEAR   True, boy. – Come, bring us to this hovel.
                                [Exeunt Lear and Kent.

FOOL   This is a brave night to cool a courtesan! I'll speak a
        prophecy ere I go: 80

            When priests are more in word than matter;
            When brewers mar their malt with water;
            When nobles are their tailors' tutors;
            No heretics burned, but wenches' suitors;
            Then shall the realm of Albion
            Come to great confusion.

            When every case in law is right;
            No squire in debt, nor no poor knight;
            When slanders do not live in tongues,
            Nor cutpurses come not to throngs;   90
            When usurers tell their gold i'th'field,
            And bawds and whores do churches build:
            Then comes the time, who lives to see't,
            That going shall be used with feet.

        This prophecy Merlin shall make, for I live before
        his time.⁹⁰   [*Exit.*

SCENE 3.

In Gloucester's house.

Enter GLOUCESTER *and* EDMUND, *with lights.*

GLO'STER   Alack, alack, Edmund, I like not this unnatural dealing.
           When I desired their leave that I might pity him, they
           took from me the use of mine own house, charged me
           on pain of perpetual displeasure neither to speak of
           him, entreat for him, or any way sustain him.

EDMUND   Most savage and unnatural!

GLO'STER   Go to; say you nothing. There is division between the
           Dukes, and a worse matter than that. I have received a
           letter this night – 'tis dangerous to be spoken – I have
           locked the letter in my closet. These injuries the King   10
           now bears will be revenged home. There is part of a
           power already footed; we must incline to the King. I
           will look him and privily relieve him; go you and

maintain talk with the Duke, that my charity be not of
him perceived; if he ask for me, I am ill and gone to
bed. If I die for it (as no less is threatened me), the King,
my old master, must be relieved. There is strange things
toward, Edmund; pray you, be careful.   [*Exit.*

EDMUND   This courtesy, forbid thee, shall the Duke
Instantly know, and of that letter too.   20
This seems a fair deserving, and must draw me
That which my father loses: no less than all.
The younger rises when the old doth fall.

                                             [*Exit.*

SCENE 4.

Outside a hovel on the heath. Storm continues.

Enter LEAR, KENT *and* FOOL.

KENT   Here is the place, my lord; good my lord, enter:
The tyranny of the open night's too rough
For nature to endure.

LEAR   Let me alone.

KENT   Good my lord, enter here.

LEAR   Wilt break my heart?

KENT   I had rather break mine own. Good my lord, enter.

LEAR   Thou think'st 'tis much that this contentious storm
Invades us to the skin: so 'tis to thee;
But where the greater malady is fixed,
The lesser is scarce felt. Thou'dst shun a bear;
But if thy flight lay toward the roaring sea,   10
Thou'dst meet the bear i'th'mouth. When the
                                   mind's free,
The body's delicate; this tempest in my mind
Doth from my senses take all feeling else
Save what beats there. Filial ingratitude:
Is it not as this mouth should tear this hand
For lifting food to't? But I will punish home.
No, I will weep no more. In such a night
To shut me out – pour on; I will endure –
In such a night as this?[91] O Regan, Goneril!

Your old kind father, whose frank heart gave all! —   20
O, that way madness lies; let me shun that!
No more of that.

KENT   Good my lord, enter here.

LEAR   Prithee go in thyself, seek thine own ease;
         This tempest will not give me leave to ponder
         On things would hurt me more. But I'll go in.
         [*To the Fool:*] In, boy, go first. — You houseless poverty
         — Nay, get thee in; I'll pray, and then I'll sleep.[92]

                                                 [*Exit Fool.*

         Poor naked wretches, whereso'er you are,
         That bide the pelting of this pitiless storm,
         How shall your houseless heads and unfed sides,   30
         Your looped and windowed raggedness, defend you
         From seasons such as these? O, I have ta'en
         Too little care of this! Take physic, pomp:
         Expose thyself to feel what wretches feel,
         That thou mayst shake the superflux to them,
         And show the heavens more just.[93]

EDGAR   [*within:*] Fathom and half, fathom and half! Poor Tom!

                    Enter the FOOL *from the hovel.*

FOOL   Come not in here, nuncle, here's a spirit. Help me,
         help me!

KENT   Give me thy hand. Who's there?   40

FOOL   A spirit, a spirit! He says his name's Poor Tom.

KENT   What art thou that dost grumble there i'th'straw?
         Come forth!

         Enter EDGAR, *as a half-naked madman, from the hovel.*

EDGAR   Away! The foul fiend follows me! Through the sharp
         hawthorn blow the cold winds. Humh! Go to thy bed
         and warm thee.

LEAR   Didst thou give all to thy daughters? And art thou
         come to this?

EDGAR   Who gives anything to Poor Tom? Whom the foul
         fiend hath led through fire and through flame, through 50
         ford and whirlpool, o'er bog and quagmire; that hath
         laid knives under his pillow and halters in his pew; set
         ratsbane by his porridge; made him proud of heart, to

ride on a bay trotting horse over four-inched bridges,
to course his own shadow for a traitor. Bless thy five
wits! Tom's a-cold. O, do de, do de, do de. Bless thee
from whirlwinds, star-blasting and taking! Do Poor
Tom some charity, whom the foul fiend vexes. There
could I have him now – and there – and there again –
and there!   [*Storm continues.* 60

LEAR   What, have his daughters brought him to this pass? –
Couldst thou save nothing? Wouldst thou give 'em all?

FOOL   Nay, he reserved a blanket; else we had been all shamed.

LEAR   [*to Edgar:*] Now all the plagues that in the pendulous air
Hang fated o'er men's faults light on thy daughters!

KENT   He hath no daughters, sir.

LEAR   Death, traitor! Nothing could have subdued nature
To such a lowness but his unkind daughters.
Is it the fashion that discarded fathers
Should have thus little mercy on their flesh?   70
Judicious punishment! 'Twas this flesh begot
Those pelican daughters.[94]

EDGAR   Pillicock sat on Pillicock Hill. Alow, alow, loo, loo!

FOOL   This cold night will turn us all to fools and madmen.

EDGAR   Take heed o'th'foul fiend. Obey thy parents, keep thy
word justly, swear not, commit not with man's sworn
spouse; set not thy sweet heart on proud array.[95] Tom's
a-cold.

LEAR   What hast thou been?

EDGAR   A serving-man, proud in heart and mind; that curled 80
my hair, wore gloves in my cap; served the lust of
my mistress' heart, and did the act of darkness with
her; swore as many oaths as I spake words, and broke
them in the sweet face of heaven; one that slept in the
contriving of lust, and waked to do it. Wine loved I
deeply, dice dearly; and in woman out-paramoured the
Turk. False of heart, light of ear, bloody of hand; hog
in sloth, fox in stealth, wolf in greediness, dog in madness, lion in prey. Let not the creaking of shoes nor the
rustling of silks betray thy poor heart to woman. Keep 90
thy foot out of brothels, thy hand out of plackets, thy
pen from lenders' books, and defy the foul fiend. Still

through the hawthorn blows the cold wind: says suum,
mun, nonny. Dolphin my boy, boy: *cessez*: let him trot
by.[96]   [*Storm continues.*

LEAR   Thou wert better in a grave than to answer with thy
uncovered body this extremity of the skies. Is man no
more than this? Consider him well. Thou ow'st the
worm no silk, the beast no hide, the sheep no wool,
the cat no perfume. Ha! Here's three on's are sophisti-   100
cated; thou art the thing itself. Unaccommodated man
is no more but such a poor, bare, forked animal as
thou art. Off, off, you lendings! Come, unbutton here.
             [*He attempts to remove his clothes, but is prevented.*

FOOL   Prithee, nuncle, be contented; 'tis a naughty night to
swim in.

                Enter GLOUCESTER *with a torch.*

Now a little fire in a wild field were like an old
lecher's heart: a small spark, all the rest on's body cold.
Look, here comes a walking fire.

EDGAR   This is the foul fiend Flibbertigibbet.[97] He begins at
curfew, and walks till the first cock. He gives the web   110
and the pin, squints the eye, and makes the harelip;
mildews the white wheat, and hurts the poor creature
of earth.
             S'Withold footed thrice the 'old;
             He met the nightmare and her ninefold,
                 Bid her alight
                 And her troth plight –
             And aroint thee, witch, aroint thee![98]

KENT   How fares your Grace?
LEAR   What's he?   120
KENT   [*to Gloucester:*] Who's there? What is't you seek?
GLO'STER   What are you there? Your names?
EDGAR   Poor Tom, that eats the swimming frog, the toad, the
tadpole, the wall-newt and the water; that in the fury
of his heart, when the foul fiend rages, eats cow-dung
for sallets, swallows the old rat and the ditch-dog,
drinks the green mantle of the standing pool; who is
whipped from tithing to tithing, and stock-punished

	and imprisoned; who hath had three suits to his back,	
	six shirts to his body,	130
	Horse to ride, and weapon to wear;	
	But mice and rats and such small deer	
	Have been Tom's food for seven long year.[99]	
	Beware my follower. Peace, Smulkin; peace, thou fiend!	
GLO'STER	What, hath your Grace no better company?	
EDGAR	The Prince of Darkness is a gentleman. Modo he's	
	called, and Mahu.[100]	
GLO'STER	Our flesh and blood, my lord, is grown so vild,	
	That it doth hate what gets it.	
EDGAR	Poor Tom's a-cold.	140
GLO'STER	[to Lear:] Go in with me; my duty cannot suffer	
	T'obey in all your daughters' hard commands.	
	Though their injunction be to bar my doors	
	And let this tyrannous night take hold upon you,	
	Yet have I ventured to come seek you out	
	And bring you where both fire and food is ready.	
LEAR	First let me talk with this philosopher.	
	[To Edgar:] What is the cause of thunder?	
KENT	Good my lord, take his offer; go into th'house.	
LEAR	I'll talk a word with this same learned Theban.[101]	150
	What is your study?	
EDGAR	How to prevent the fiend and to kill vermin.	
LEAR	Let me ask you one word in private.	
KENT	Impórtune him once more to go, my lord;	
	His wits begin t'unsettle. [Storm continues.	
GLO'STER	Canst thou blame him?	
	His daughters seek his death. Ah, that good Kent,	
	He said it would be thus, poor banished man!	
	Thou say'st the King grows mad; I'll tell thee, friend,	
	I am almost mad myself. I had a son,	
	Now outlawed from my blood: he sought my life	160
	But lately, very late. I loved him, friend,	
	No father his son dearer: true to tell thee,	
	The grief hath crazed my wits. What a night's this!	
	[To Lear:] I do beseech your Grace –	
LEAR	O cry you mercy, sir.	
	[To Edgar:] Noble philosopher, your company.	

EDGAR   Tom's a-cold.

GLO'STER   In, fellow, there, into th'hovel; keep thee warm.

LEAR   Come, let's in all.

KENT   This way, my lord.

LEAR   With him;
           I will keep still with my philosopher.

KENT   Good my lord, soothe him; let him take the fellow.   170

GLO'STER   Take him you on.

KENT   Sirrah, come on; go along with us.

LEAR   Come, good Athenian.[102]

GLO'STER   No words, no words; hush!

EDGAR   Childe Rowland to the dark tower came.
               His word was still 'Fie, foh, and fum;
               I smell the blood of a British man.'[103]   [*Exeunt.*

SCENE 5.

In Gloucester's house.

Enter CORNWALL *and* EDMUND.

CORNWALL I will have my revenge ere I depart his house.

EDMUND   How, my lord, I may be censured, that nature thus
         gives way to loyalty, something fears me to think of.

CORNWALL I now perceive it was not altogether your brother's evil
         disposition made him seek his death, but a provoking
         merit, set a-work by a reprovable badness in himself.[104]

EDMUND   How malicious is my fortune, that I must repent to be
         just! This is the letter he spoke of, which approves him
         an intelligent party to the advantages of France.[105] O
         heavens! That this treason were not – or not I the   10
         detector!

CORNWALL Go with me to the Duchess.

EDMUND   If the matter of this paper be certain, you have mighty
         business in hand.

CORNWALL True or false, it hath made thee Earl of Gloucester.
         Seek out where thy father is, that he may be ready for
         our apprehension.

EDMUND   [*aside:*] If I find him comforting the King, it will stuff

his suspicion more fully. [*To Cornwall:*] I will perséver
in my course of loyalty, though the conflict be sore 20
between that and my blood.

CORNWALL I will lay trust upon thee; and thou shalt find a dearer
father in my love.   [*Exeunt.*

SCENE 6.

In an outbuilding of Gloucester's house.

Enter GLOUCESTER *and* KENT.

GLO'STER Here is better than the open air; take it thankfully. I
will piece out the comfort with what addition I can. I
will not be long from you.

KENT All the power of his wits have given way to his impatience. The gods reward your kindness!
    [*Exit Gloucester.*

Enter LEAR, EDGAR *and* FOOL.

EDGAR Frateretto calls me, and tells me Nero is an angler in
the lake of darkness.[106] Pray, innocent, and beware the
foul fiend.

FOOL Prithee, nuncle, tell me whether a madman be a gentleman or a yeoman.   10

LEAR A king, a king!

FOOL No, he's a yeoman that has a gentleman to his son; for
he's a mad yeoman that sees his son a gentleman before
him.[107]

LEAR To have a thousand with red burning spits
Come hizzing in upon 'em!

EDGAR The foul fiend bites my back.

FOOL He's mad that trusts in the tameness of a wolf, a horse's
health, a boy's love, or a whore's oath.

LEAR It shall be done; I will arraign them straight.   20
[*To Edgar:*] Come, sit thou here, most learnèd justicer;
[*to the Fool:*]
Thou sapient sir, sit here. No, you she-foxes –

EDGAR Look where he stands and glares! Want'st thou eyes at
trial, madam?

	[*Sings:*] Come o'er the bourn, Bessy, to me.[108]
FOOL	[*sings:*] Her boat hath a leak,
	And she must not speak
	Why she dares not come over to thee.
EDGAR	The foul fiend haunts Poor Tom in the voice of a nightingale. Hoppedance cries in Tom's belly for two white herring. Croak not, black angel; I have no food for thee.[109]
KENT	[*to Lear:*] How do you, sir? Stand you not so amazed. Will you lie down and rest upon the cushions?
LEAR	I'll see their trial first. Bring in their evidence.
	[*To Edgar:*] Thou robèd man of justice, take thy place;
	[*to the Fool:*] And thou, his yokefellow of equity,
	Bench by his side.
	[*To Kent:*] You are o'th'commission;
	Sit you too.
EDGAR	Let us deal justly.
	Sleepest or wakest thou, jolly shepherd?
	Thy sheep be in the corn;
	And for one blast of thy minikin mouth
	Thy sheep shall take no harm.
	Purr the cat is grey.[110]
LEAR	Arraign her first: 'tis Goneril — I here take my oath before this honourable assembly — kicked the poor King, her father.
FOOL	Come hither, mistress; is your name Goneril?
LEAR	She cannot deny it.
FOOL	Cry you mercy, I took you for a joint-stool.
LEAR	And here's another, whose warped looks proclaim What stone her heart is made on. Stop her there! Arms, arms, sword, fire! Corruption in the place! False justicer, why hast thou let her scape?[111]
EDGAR	Bless thy five wits!
KENT	O pity! Sir, where is the patience now That you so oft have boasted to retain?
EDGAR	[*aside:*] My tears begin to take his part so much, They mar my counterfeiting.
LEAR	The little dogs and all, Trey, Blanch, and Sweetheart, see, they bark at me.

Line numbers in margin: 30, 40, 50, 60

EDGAR   Tom will throw his head at them. Avaunt, you curs!
                    Be thy mouth or black or white,
                    Tooth that poisons if it bite;
                    Mastiff, greyhound, mongrel grim,
                    Hound or spaniel, brach or him,[112]
                    Or bobtail tyke or trundle-tail,
                    Tom will make him weep and wail;
                    For, with throwing thus my head,   70
                    Dogs leap the hatch, and all are fled.
            Do, de, de, de. *Cessez*! Come, march to wakes and
            fairs and market towns. Poor Tom, thy horn is dry.
LEAR   Then let them anatomize Regan; see what breeds
            about her heart. Is there any cause in nature that makes
            these hard hearts? [*To Edgar:*] You, sir, I entertain for
            one of my hundred; only I do not like the fashion of
            your garments. You will say they are Persian;[113] but let
            them be changed.
KENT   Now good my lord, lie here and rest awhile.   80
LEAR   Make no noise, make no noise; draw the curtains. So,
            so; we'll go to supper i'th'morning.
FOOL   And I'll go to bed at noon.[114]   [*Lear sleeps.*

                         Enter GLOUCESTER.

GLO'STER   Come hither, friend. Where is the King my master?
KENT   Here, sir; but trouble him not: his wits are gone.
GLO'STER   Good friend, I prithee take him in thy arms.
            I have o'erheard a plot of death upon him.
            There is a litter ready; lay him in't,
            And drive toward Dover, friend, where thou shalt meet
            Both welcome and protection. Take up thy master;   90
            If thou should'st dally half an hour, his life,
            With thine, and all that offer to defend him,
            Stand in assurèd loss. Take up, take up
            And follow me, that will to some provision
            Give thee quick conduct.
KENT   Oppressed nature sleeps. –
            This rest might yet have balmed thy broken sinews,
            Which, if convenience will not allow,
            Stand in hard cure.
            [*To the Fool:*]   Come, help to bear thy master;

Thou must not stay behind.[115]

GLO'STER   Come, come, away!

[*Exeunt all but Edgar.*

EDGAR   When we our betters see bearing our woes,   100
We scarcely think our miseries our foes.
Who alone suffers, suffers most i'th'mind,
Leaving free things and happy shows behind;
But then the mind much sufferance doth o'erskip
When grief hath mates, and bearing fellowship.
How light and portable my pain seems now,
When that which makes me bend makes the King bow.
He childed as I fathered! Tom, away!
Mark the high noises, and thyself bewray
When false opinion, whose wrong thoughts defile thee,   110
In thy just proof repeals and reconciles thee.[116]
What will hap more tonight, safe scape the King!
Lurk, lurk.[117]   [*Exit.*

SCENE 7.

A room in Gloucester's house.

Enter CORNWALL, REGAN, GONERIL, EDMUND *and* SERVANTS.

CORNWALL [*to Goneril:*] Post speedily to my lord your husband;
show him this letter: the army of France is landed. –
Seek out the traitor Gloucester!   [*Exeunt some servants.*
REGAN   Hang him instantly.
GONERIL Pluck out his eyes.
CORNWALL Leave him to my displeasure. Edmund, keep you our
sister company: the revenges we are bound to take
upon your traitorous father are not fit for your behold-
ing. Advise the Duke, where you are going, to a most
festinate preparation: we are bound to the like. Our   10
posts shall be swift and intelligent betwixt us. Farewell,
dear sister; farewell, my lord of Gloucester.

Enter OSWALD.

How now? Where's the King?
OSWALD   My lord of Gloucester hath conveyed him hence.

Some five- or six-and-thirty of his knights,
Hot questrists after him, met him at gate,
Who, with some other of the lord's dependants,
Are gone with him toward Dover, where they boast
To have well-armed friends.

CORNWALL　　　　　　　　　　　Get horses for your mistress.

GONERIL　Farewell, sweet lord, and sister.　　　　　　　　20

CORNWALL　Edmund, farewell. [*Exeunt Goneril, Edmund and Oswald.*
　　　　　　　　　　Go seek the traitor Gloucester;
Pinion him like a thief; bring him before us.
　　　　　　　　　　　　　[*Exeunt servants.*
Though well we may not pass upon his life
Without the form of justice, yet our power
Shall do a court'sy to our wrath, which men
May blame, but not control.

　　　　　Enter SERVANTS *with* GLOUCESTER.

　　　　　　　　　　Who's there? The traitor?

REGAN　Ingrateful fox! – 'Tis he.

CORNWALL　Bind fast his corky arms.

GLO'STER　What means your Graces? Good my friends, consider:
You are my guests. Do me no foul play, friends.　　　30

CORNWALL　Bind him, I say.　　　　　　[*Servants bind Gloucester.*

REGAN　　　　　　　　　Hard, hard. – O filthy traitor!

GLO'STER　Unmerciful lady as you are, I'm none.

CORNWALL　To this chair bind him. Villain, thou shalt find –
　　　　　　　　　　　　[*Regan plucks Gloucester's beard.*

GLO'STER　By the kind gods, 'tis most ignobly done
To pluck me by the beard.

REGAN　So white, and such a traitor?

GLO'STER　　　　　　　　　　Naughty lady,
These hairs which thou dost ravish from my chin
Will quicken and accuse thee. I am your host:
With robbers' hands my hospitable favours
You should not ruffle thus. What will you do?　　　40

CORNWALL　Come, sir. What letters had you late from France?

REGAN　Be simple-answered, for we know the truth.

CORNWALL　And what confederacy have you with the traitors
Late footed in the kingdom –

REGAN　　　　　　　　　　To whose hands

	You have sent the lunatic King? Speak.
GLO'STER	I have a letter, guessingly set down,

GLO'STER   I have a letter, guessingly set down,
          Which came from one that's of a neutral heart,
          And not from one opposed.

CORNWALL   Cunning.

REGAN   And false.

CORNWALL Where hast thou sent the King?

GLO'STER   To Dover.

REGAN   Wherefore to Dover? Wast thou not charged at peril –   50

CORNWALL Wherefore to Dover? Let him answer that.

GLO'STER   I am tied to th'stake, and I must stand the course.

REGAN   Wherefore to Dover?

GLO'STER   Because I would not see thy cruel nails
          Pluck out his poor old eyes, nor thy fierce sister
          In his anointed flesh stick boarish fangs.[118]
          The sea, with such a storm as his bare head
          In hell-black night endured, would have buoyed up,
          And quenched the stellèd fires;
          Yet, poor old heart, he holp the heavens to rain.[119]   60
          If wolves had at thy gate howled that stern time,
          Thou should'st have said 'Good porter, turn the key';
          All cruels else subscribe;[120] but I shall see
          The wingèd vengeance overtake such children.

CORNWALL See't shalt thou never. – Fellows, hold the chair. –
          Upon these eyes of thine I'll set my foot.

GLO'STER   He that will think to live till he be old,
          Give me some help.
          [*Cornwall gouges one eye.*] O cruel! O you gods!

REGAN   One side will mock another. Th'other too!

CORNWALL If you see vengeance –

SERVANT 1   Hold your hand, my lord!   70
          I have served you ever since I was a child,
          But better service have I never done you
          Than now to bid you hold.

REGAN   How now, you dog?

SERVANT 1 If you did wear a beard upon your chin,
          I'd shake it on this quarrel.

REGAN   What do you mean?

CORNWALL My villain?   [*Cornwall and servant draw their swords.*

SERVANT 1 Nay, then, come on, and take the chance of anger.
                               [They fight. Cornwall is wounded.

REGAN   *[to another servant:]* Give me thy sword. A peasant
                                           stand up thus?
                   [She takes a sword and runs at him behind.

SERVANT 1 O, I am slain! My lord, you have one eye left
           To see some mischief on him. O!   *[He dies.* 80

CORNWALL Lest it see more, prevent it. Out, vild jelly!
                   [He gouges Gloucester's remaining eye.
           Where is thy lustre now?

GLO'STER All dark and comfortless! Where's my son Edmund?
           Edmund, enkindle all the sparks of nature
           To quit this horrid act.

REGAN   Out, treacherous villain:
           Thou call'st on him that hates thee. It was he
           That made the overture of thy treasons to us,
           Who is too good to pity thee.

GLO'STER O, my follies! Then Edgar was abused.
           Kind gods, forgive me that, and prosper him!   90

REGAN Go thrust him out at gates, and let him smell
           His way to Dover.   *[Servant leads Gloucester away.*
                   How is 't, my lord? How look you?

CORNWALL I have received a hurt. Follow me, lady.
           – Turn out that eyeless villain. Throw this slave
           Upon the dunghill. – Regan, I bleed apace.
           Untimely comes this hurt. Give me your arm.
                   [Exeunt Cornwall and Regan.

SERVANT 2 I'll never care what wickedness I do,
           If this man come to good.

SERVANT 3   If she live long,
           And in the end meet the old course of death,
           Women will all turn monsters.   100

SERVANT 2 Let's follow the old Earl, and get the bedlam
           To lead him where he would; his roguish madness
           Allows itself to anything.

SERVANT 3 Go thou; I'll fetch some flax and whites of eggs
           To apply to his bleeding face. Now heaven help him![121]
                                         [Exeunt.

ACT 4, SCENE 1.

The heath.

Enter EDGAR, *still disguised as Poor Tom.*

EDGAR Yet better thus, and known to be contemned,
Than still contemned and flattered. To be worst,
The lowest and most dejected thing of Fortune,
Stands still in esperance, lives not in fear.
The lamentable change is from the best;
The worst returns to laughter. Welcome, then,
Thou unsubstantial air that I embrace:
The wretch that thou hast blown unto the worst
Owes nothing to thy blasts.[122]

Enter GLOUCESTER, *led by an* OLD MAN.

                              But who comes here?
My father, poorly led![123] World, world, O world!   10
But that thy strange mutations make us hate thee,
Life would not yield to age.[124]

OLD MAN   O my good lord,
I have been your tenant, and your father's tenant,
These fourscore years.

GLO'STER Away, get thee away! Good friend, be gone:
Thy comforts can do me no good at all;
Thee they may hurt.

OLD MAN   You cannot see your way.

GLO'STER I have no way, and therefore want no eyes;
I stumbled when I saw. Full oft 'tis seen
Our means secure us, and our mere defects   20
Prove our commodities.[125] O dear son Edgar,
The food of thy abusèd father's wrath!
Might I but live to see thee in my touch,
I'd say I had eyes again

OLD MAN   How now? Who's there?

EDGAR [*aside:*] O gods! Who is't can say 'I am at the worst'?
I am worse than e'er I was –

OLD MAN   'Tis poor mad Tom.

EDGAR   And worse I may be yet: the worst is not
            So long as we can say 'This is the worst'.
OLD MAN   Fellow, where goest?
GLO'STER   Is it a beggar-man?
OLD MAN   Madman, and beggar too.   30
GLO'STER   He has some reason, else he could not beg.
            I'th'last night's storm, I such a fellow saw,
            Which made me think a man a worm. My son
            Came then into my mind, and yet my mind
            Was then scarce friends with him; I have heard more
                                                          since.
            As flies to wanton boys are we to the gods:
            They kill us for their sport.
EDGAR   [aside:]   How should this be?
            Bad is the trade that must play Fool to sorrow,
            Ang'ring itself and others. – Bless thee, master!
GLO'STER   Is that the naked fellow?
OLD MAN   Ay, my lord.   40
GLO'STER   Then prithee get thee away. If, for my sake,
            Thou wilt o'ertake us hence a mile or twain
            I'th'way toward Dover, do it for ancient love;
            And bring some covering for this naked soul
            Which I'll entreat to lead me.
OLD MAN   Alack, sir, he is mad!
GLO'STER   'Tis the time's plague when madmen lead the blind.
            Do as I bid thee; or rather do thy pleasure:
            Above the rest, be gone.
OLD MAN   I'll bring him the best 'parel that I have,
            Come on't what will.   [Exit.
GLO'STER   Sirrah, naked fellow!   50
EDGAR   Poor Tom's a-cold. [Aside:] I cannot daub it further –
GLO'STER   Come hither, fellow.
EDGAR   And yet I must. – Bless thy sweet eyes, they bleed!
GLO'STER   Know'st thou the way to Dover?
EDGAR   Both stile and gate, horseway and footpath. Poor Tom
            hath been scared out of his good wits. Bless thee, good
            man's son, from the foul fiend! Five fiends have been in
            Poor Tom at once: as Obidicut, of lust; Hobbididence,
            Prince of Darkness; Mahu, of stealing; Modo, of murder;

Flibbertigibbet, of mocking and mowing, who since 60
possesses chambermaids and waiting-women. So, bless
thee, master![126]

GLO'STER Here, take this purse, thou whom the heavens' plagues
Have humbled to all strokes: that I am wretched
Makes thee the happier. Heavens, deal so still!
Let the superfluous and lust-dieted man,
That slaves your ordinance,[127] that will not see
Because he does not feel, feel your power quickly:
So distribution should undo excess,
And each man have enough. Dost thou know Dover?   70

EDGAR   Ay, master.

GLO'STER There is a cliff, whose high and bending head
Looks fearfully in the confinèd deep.
Bring me but to the very brim of it,
And I'll repair the misery thou dost bear
With something rich about me. From that place
I shall no leading need.

EDGAR   Give me thy arm;
Poor Tom shall lead thee.   [Exeunt.

SCENE 2.

Outside the Duke of Albany's house.

Enter GONERIL *and* EDMUND.

GONERIL   Welcome, my lord. I marvel our mild husband
Not met us on the way.

Enter OSWALD.

                             Now, where's your master?

OSWALD   Madam, within; but never man so changed.
I told him of the army that was landed;
He smiled at it. I told him you were coming;
His answer was, 'The worse'. Of Gloucester's treachery
And of the loyal service of his son,
When I informed him, then he called me 'sot'
And told me I had turned the wrong side out.
What most he should dislike seems pleasant to him;   10

What like, offensive.

GONERIL   [*to Edmund:*]   Then shall you go no further.
It is the cowish terror of his spirit,
That dares not undertake; he'll not feel wrongs
Which tie him to an answer. Our wishes on the way
May prove effects.[128] Back, Edmund, to my brother;
Hasten his musters and conduct his powers.
I must change arms at home and give the distaff
Into my husband's hands.[129] This trusty servant
Shall pass between us: ere long you are like to hear
(If you dare venture in your own behalf)   20
A mistress's command. Wear this. [*She gives a favour.*]
                                                    Spare speech;
Decline your head: this kiss, if it durst speak,
Would stretch thy spirits up into the air.
Conceive, and fare thee well.

EDMUND   Yours in the ranks of death!

GONERIL   My most dear Gloucester!
                                                    [*Exit Edmund.*

O, the difference of man and man!
To thee a woman's services are due;
A fool usurps my bed.[130]

OSWALD   Madam, here comes my lord.
                                                    [*Exit.*

                          Enter ALBANY.

GONERIL   I have been worth the whistling.

ALBANY   O Goneril,
You are not worth the dust which the rude wind   30
Blows in your face! I fear your disposition.
That nature which contemns its origin
Cannot be bordered certain in itself.
She that herself will sliver and disbranch
From her material sap, perforce must wither
And come to deadly use.

GONERIL   No more; the text is foolish.

ALBANY   Wisdom and goodness to the vild seem vild;
Filths savour but themselves.[131] What have you done?
Tigers, not daughters, what have you performed?   40

A father, and a gracious agèd man,
Whose reverence even the head-lugged bear would lick,
Most barbarous, most degenerate, have you madded.
Could my good brother suffer you to do it?
A man, a prince, by him so benefited!
If that the heavens do not their visible spirits
Send quickly down to tame these vild offences,
It will come,
Humanity must perforce prey on itself
Like monsters of the deep.[132]

GONERIL   Milk-livered man,   50
That bear'st a cheek for blows, a head for wrongs,
Who hast not in thy brows an eye discerning
Thine honour from thy suffering; that not know'st
Fools do those villains pity who are punished
Ere they have done their mischief. Where's thy drum?
France spreads his banners in our noiseless land,
With plumèd helm thy state begins to threat,
Whilst thou, a moral fool, sits still and cries
'Alack, why does he so?'[133]

ALBANY   See thyself, devil!
Proper deformity shows not in the fiend   60
So horrid as in woman.

GONERIL   O vain fool!

ALBANY   Thou changèd and self-covered thing,[134] for shame
Be-monster not thy feature. Were't my fitness
To let these hands obey my blood,
They are apt enough to dislocate and tear
Thy flesh and bones. Howe'er thou art a fiend,
A woman's shape doth shield thee.

GONERIL   Marry, your manhood! Mew![135]

Enter a MESSENGER.

ALBANY   What news?[136]

MESSENGER   O, my good lord, the Duke of Cornwall's dead,   70
Slain by his servant, going to put out
The other eye of Gloucester.

ALBANY   Gloucester's eyes!

MESSENGER A servant that he bred, thrilled with remorse,

Opposed against the act, bending his sword
To his great master; who, thereat enraged,
Flew on him, and amongst them felled him dead;
But not without that harmful stroke which since
Hath plucked him after.

ALBANY   This shows you are above,
You justicers, that these our nether crimes
So speedily can venge! But (O poor Gloucester!)   80
Lost he his other eye?

MESSENGER   Both, both, my lord. –
This letter, madam, craves a speedy answer;
'Tis from your sister.   [*He presents a letter.*

GONERIL [*aside:*]   One way I like this well;
But being widow, and my Gloucester with her,
May all the building in my fancy pluck
Upon my hateful life. Another way
The news is not so tart.[137] – I'll read, and answer.
                              [*Exit.*

ALBANY   Where was his son when they did take his eyes?
MESSENGER Come with my lady hither.
ALBANY   He is not here.
MESSENGER No, my good lord; I met him back again.   90
ALBANY   Knows he the wickedness?
MESSENGER Ay, my good lord: 'twas he informed against him,
And quit the house on purpose that their punishment
Might have the freer course.
ALBANY   Gloucester, I live
To thank thee for the love thou show'dst the King,
And to revenge thine eyes. Come hither, friend;
Tell me what more thou know'st.   [*Exeunt.*

SCENE 3.[138]

The French camp near Dover.

Enter KENT *and a* GENTLEMAN.

KENT　Why the King of France is so suddenly gone back,
know you no reason?

GENT.　Something he left imperfect in the state, which since
his coming forth is thought of, which imports to the
kingdom so much fear and danger that his personal
return was most required and necessary.

KENT　Who hath he left behind him General?

GENT.　The Marshal of France, Monsieur la Far.

KENT　Did your letters pierce the Queen to any demonstra-
tion of grief?　　　　　　　　　　　　　　　　　　　　　10

GENT.　Ay, sir; she took them, read them in my presence,
And now and then an ample tear trilled down
Her delicate cheek. It seemed she was a queen
Over her passion, who, most rebel-like,
Sought to be king o'er her.

KENT　　　　　　　　　　　　O, then it moved her.

GENT.　Not to a rage; patience and sorrow strove
Who should express her goodliest. You have seen
Sunshine and rain at once; her smiles and tears
Were like, a better way: those happy smilets
That played on her ripe lip seemed not to know　　　20
What guests were in her eyes, which parted thence
As pearls from diamonds dropped. In brief,
Sorrow would be a rarity most beloved
If all could so become it.

KENT　　　　　　　　　　　Made she no verbal question?

GENT.　Faith, once or twice she heaved the name of father
Pantingly forth, as if it pressed her heart;
Cried 'Sisters, sisters! Shame of ladies! Sisters!
Kent! Father! Sisters! What, i'th'storm, i'th'night?
Let pity not believe it!'[139] There she shook
The holy water from her heavenly eyes　　　　　　　30
That clamour moistened;[140] then away she started,

To deal with grief alone.

KENT   It is the stars,
The stars above us, govern our conditions;
Else one self mate and make could not beget
Such different issues. You spoke not with her since?

GENT.   No.

KENT   Was this before the King returned?

GENT.   No, since.

KENT   Well, sir, the poor distressèd Lear's i'th'town,
Who sometime, in his better tune, remembers
What we are come about, and by no means   40
Will yield to see his daughter.

GENT.   Why, good sir?

KENT   A sovereign shame so elbows him: his own unkindness,
That stripped her from his benediction, turned her
To foreign casualties, gave her dear rights
To his dog-hearted daughters – these things sting
His mind so venomously that burning shame
Detains him from Cordelia.

GENT.   Alack, poor gentleman!

KENT   Of Albany's and Cornwall's powers you heard not?

GENT.   'Tis so; they are afoot.

KENT   Well, sir, I'll bring you to our master, Lear,   50
And leave you to attend him. Some dear cause
Will in concealment wrap me up awhile;
When I am known aright, you shall not grieve
Lending me this acquaintance. I pray you go
Along with me.   [*Exeunt.*

SCENE 4.

The French camp.

Enter, with drum and colours, CORDELIA, DOCTOR *and* SOLDIERS.

CORDELIA   Alack, 'tis he! Why, he was met even now,
           As mad as the vexed sea, singing aloud,
           Crowned with rank femiter and furrow-weeds,
           With hardocks, hemlock, nettles, cuckoo-flowers,
           Darnel, and all the idle weeds that grow
           In our sustaining corn. A century send forth:
           Search every acre in the high-grown field,
           And bring him to our eye.   [*Exeunt some soldiers.*
                              What can man's wisdom
           In the restoring his bereavèd sense?
           He that helps him, take all my outward worth.[141]   10
DOCTOR   There is means, madam.
           Our foster-nurse of nature is repose,
           The which he lacks. That to provoke in him
           Are many simples operative, whose power
           Will close the eye of anguish.
CORDELIA   All blest secrets,
           All you unpublished virtues of the earth,
           Spring with my tears; be aidant and remediate
           In the good man's distress! – Seek, seek for him,
           Lest his ungoverned rage dissolve the life
           That wants the means to lead it.

Enter MESSENGER.

MESSENGER   News, madam!   20
           The British powers are marching hitherward.
CORDELIA   'Tis known before: our preparation stands
           In expectation of them. O dear father,
           It is thy business that I go about;[142]
           Therefore great France
           My mourning and important tears hath pitied.
           No blown ambition doth our arms incite,
           But love, dear love, and our aged father's right.
           Soon may I hear and see him!   [*Exeunt.*

SCENE 5.

Gloucester's house.

Enter REGAN *and* OSWALD.

REGAN	But are my brother's powers set forth?
OSWALD	Ay, madam.
REGAN	Himself in person there?
OSWALD	Madam, with much ado.
	Your sister is the better soldier.
REGAN	Lord Edmund spake not with your lord at home?
OSWALD	No, madam.
REGAN	What might import my sister's letter to him?
OSWALD	I know not, lady.
REGAN	Faith, he is posted hence on serious matter.
	It was great ignorance, Gloucester's eyes being out,
	To let him live: where he arrives he moves 10
	All hearts against us. Edmund, I think, is gone,
	In pity of his misery, to dispatch
	His nighted life; moreover, to descry
	The strength o'th'enemy.
OSWALD	I must needs after him, madam, with my letter.
REGAN	Our troops set forth tomorrow. Stay with us;
	The ways are dangerous.
OSWALD	I may not, madam;
	My lady charged my duty in this business.
REGAN	Why should she write to Edmund? Might not you
	Transport her purposes by word? Belike, 20
	Some things, I know not what.[143] I'll love thee much:
	Let me unseal the letter.
OSWALD	Madam, I had rather –
REGAN	I know your lady does not love her husband;
	I am sure of that; and at her late being here,
	She gave strange eliads and most speaking looks
	To noble Edmund. I know you are of her bosom.
OSWALD	I, madam?
REGAN	I speak in understanding: y'are: I know't;
	Therefore I do advise you take this note.

My lord is dead; Edmund and I have talked,   30
And more convenient is he for my hand
Than for your lady's. You may gather more.
If you do find him, pray you give him this;[144]
And when your mistress hears thus much from you,
I pray desire her call her wisdom to her.
So fare you well.
If you do chance to hear of that blind traitor,
Preferment falls on him that cuts him off.

OSWALD   Would I could meet him, madam: I should show
What party I do follow.

REGAN   Fare thee well.   40

                              [*Exeunt separately*.

SCENE 6.

The countryside near Dover.

Enter EDGAR, *dressed like a peasant, leading* GLOUCESTER.

GLO'STER   When shall I come to th'top of that same hill?
EDGAR   You do climb up it now. Look how we labour.
GLO'STER   Methinks the ground is even.
EDGAR   Horrible steep.
Hark, do you hear the sea?
GLO'STER   No, truly.
EDGAR   Why, then your other senses grow imperfect
By your eyes' anguish.
GLO'STER   So may it be indeed.
Methinks thy voice is altered, and thou speak'st
In better phrase and matter than thou didst.
EDGAR   Y'are much deceived: in nothing am I changed
But in my garments.
GLO'STER   Methinks y'are better spoken.   10
EDGAR   Come on, sir, here's the place. Stand still; how fearful
And dizzy 'tis to cast one's eyes so low!
The crows and choughs that wing the midway air
Show scarce so gross as beetles. Half-way down
Hangs one that gathers sampire – dreadful trade!
Methinks he seems no bigger than his head.

The fishermen that walk upon the beach
Appear like mice, and yond tall anchoring bark
Diminished to her cock, her cock a buoy
Almost too small for sight. The murmuring surge,   20
That on th'unnumbered idle pebble chafes,
Cannot be heard so high. I'll look no more,
Lest my brain turn and the deficient sight
Topple down headlong.[145]

GLO'STER   Set me where you stand.

EDGAR   Give me your hand. You are now within a foot
Of th'extreme verge. For all beneath the moon
Would I not leap upright.

GLO'STER   Let go my hand.
Here, friend, 's another purse, in it a jewel
Well worth a poor man's taking. Fairies and gods
Prosper it with thee! Go thou further off;   30
Bid me farewell, and let me hear thee going.

EDGAR   Now fare ye well, good sir.

GLO'STER   With all my heart!

EDGAR   [*aside:*] Why I do trifle thus with his despair
Is done to cure it.

GLO'STER   O you mighty gods!
This world I do renounce, and in your sights
Shake patiently my great affliction off.
If I could bear it longer, and not fall
To quarrel with your great opposeless wills,
My snuff and loathèd part of nature should
Burn itself out.[146] If Edgar live, O bless him!   40
Now, fellow, fare thee well.

EDGAR   Gone, sir; farewell!
          [*Gloucester falls forward, and remains prone.*
[*Aside:*] And yet I know not how conceit may rob
The treasury of life, when life itself
Yields to the theft. Had he been where he thought,
By this had thought been past. Alive, or dead?
[*Aloud:*] Ho, you sir! Friend! Hear you, sir? Speak!
[*Aside:*] Thus might he pass indeed; yet he revives.
[*Aloud:*] What are you, sir?

GLO'STER   Away, and let me die.

EDGAR   Hadst thou been aught but gosmore, feathers, air
             (So many fathom down precipitating),   50
             Thou'dst shivered like an egg; but thou dost breathe,
             Hast heavy substance, bleed'st not, speak'st, art sound.
             Ten masts at each make not the altitude
             Which thou hast perpendicularly fell.
             Thy life's a miracle. Speak yet again.

GLO'STER   But have I fall'n, or no?

EDGAR   From the dread summit of this chalky bourn.
             Look up a-height: the shrill-gorged lark so far
             Cannot be seen, or heard. Do but look up.

GLO'STER   Alack, I have no eyes.   60
             Is wretchedness deprived that benefit
             To end itself by death? 'Twas yet some comfort
             When misery could beguile the tyrant's rage
             And frustrate his proud will.

EDGAR   Give me your arm.
             Up; so. How is't? Feel you your legs? You stand.

GLO'STER   Too well, too well.

EDGAR   This is above all strangeness.
             Upon the crown o'th'cliff, what thing was that
             Which parted from you?

GLO'STER   A poor unfortunate beggar.

EDGAR   As I stood here below, methought his eyes
             Were two full moons; he had a thousand noses,   70
             Horns whelked and waved like the enragèd sea:[147]
             It was some fiend. Therefore, thou happy father,
             Think that the clearest gods, who make them honours
             Of men's impossibilities,[148] have preserved thee.

GLO'STER   I do remember now. Henceforth I'll bear
             Affliction till it do cry out itself
             'Enough, enough', and die. That thing you speak of,
             I took it for a man. Often 'twould say
             'The fiend, the fiend'; he led me to that place.

EDGAR   Bear free and patient thoughts.

             Enter LEAR, *mad, crowned with wild flowers and weeds.*

                                        But who comes here?   80
             The safer sense will ne'er accommodate
             His master thus.[149]

LEAR   No, they cannot touch me for coining; I am the King himself.

EDGAR   O thou side-piercing sight!

LEAR   Nature's above art in that respect. There's your press-money. That fellow handles his bow like a crow-keeper; draw me a clothier's yard. Look, look, a mouse! Peace, peace; this piece of toasted cheese will do't. There's my gauntlet; I'll prove it on a giant. Bring up the brown 90 bills. O, well flown, bird; i'th'clout, i'th'clout: hewgh![150] Give the word.

EDGAR   Sweet marjoram.

LEAR   Pass.

GLO'STER   I know that voice.

LEAR   Ha! Goneril with a white beard? They flattered me like a dog, and told me I had the white hairs in my beard ere the black ones were there. To say 'ay' and 'no' to everything that I said 'ay' and 'no' to was no good divinity.[151] When the rain came to wet me once and 100 the wind to make me chatter, when the thunder would not peace at my bidding, there I found 'em, there I smelt 'em out! Go to, they are not men o' their words: they told me I was everything; 'tis a lie – I am not ague-proof.

GLO'STER   The trick of that voice I do well remember:
          Is't not the King?

LEAR   Ay, every inch a king!
When I do stare, see how the subject quakes.
I pardon that man's life. What was thy cause?
Adultery?   110
Thou shalt not die. Die for adultery? No!
The wren goes to't, and the small gilded fly
Does lecher in my sight.
Let copulation thrive: for Gloucester's bastard son
Was kinder to his father than my daughters
Got 'tween the lawful sheets.
To't, luxury, pell-mell, for I lack soldiers!
Behold yond simp'ring dame
Whose face between her forks presages snow,
That minces virtue[152] and does shake the head   120

To hear of pleasure's name;
The fitchew nor the soiled horse goes to't
With a more riotous appetite.
Down from the waist they are centaurs,
Though women all above.
But to the girdle do the gods inherit;
Beneath is all the fiend's.
There's hell, there's darkness, there's the sulphurous pit;
Burning, scalding, stench, consumption.
Fie, fie, fie; pah, pah!   130
Give me an ounce of civet; good apothecary,
Sweeten my imagination: there's money for thee.[153]

GLO'STER   O, let me kiss that hand!

LEAR   Let me wipe it first; it smells of mortality.

GLO'STER   O ruined piece of Nature! This great world
            Shall so wear out to naught. Dost thou know me?

LEAR   I remember thine eyes well enough. Dost thou squiny
            at me?
            No, do thy worst, blind Cupid; I'll not love.
            Read thou this challenge: mark but the penning of it.   140

GLO'STER   Were all thy letters suns, I could not see.

EDGAR   [aside:] I would not take this from report. It is,
            And my heart breaks at it.

LEAR   Read.

GLO'STER   What! With the case of eyes?

LEAR   O ho, are you there with me? No eyes in your head, nor
            no money in your purse? Your eyes are in a heavy case,
            your purse in a light; yet you see how this world goes.

GLO'STER   I see it feelingly.

LEAR   What, art mad? A man may see how this world goes, 150
            with no eyes. Look with thine ears: see how yond
            justice rails upon yond simple thief. Hark in thine ear:
            change places and, handy-dandy, which is the justice,
            which is the thief? Thou hast seen a farmer's dog bark
            at a beggar?

GLO'STER   Ay, sir.

LEAR   And the creature run from the cur? There thou
            mightst behold the great image of authority: a dog's
            obeyed in office.

| | Thou rascal beadle, hold thy bloody hand! | 160 |

Thou rascal beadle, hold thy bloody hand!   160
Why dost thou lash that whore? Strip thy own back;
Thou hotly lusts to use her in that kind
For which thou whipp'st her. The usurer hangs the
                                                    cozener.
Through tattered clothes great vices do appear;
Robes and furred gowns hide all. Plate sin with gold,
And the strong lance of justice hurtless breaks;
Arm it in rags, a pigmy's straw does pierce it.
None does offend, none, I say none. I'll able 'em.
Take that of me, my friend, who have the power
To seal th'accuser's lips.[154] Get thee glass eyes   170
And, like a scurvy politician, seem
To see the things thou dost not.[155] Now, now, now,
Now. Pull off my boots: harder, harder! So.

EDGAR   [aside:] O, matter and impertinency mixed:
Reason in madness!

LEAR   If thou wilt weep my fortunes, take my eyes.
I know thee well enough: thy name is Gloucester.
Thou must be patient. We came crying hither:
Thou know'st, the first time that we smell the air,
We wawl and cry. I will preach to thee: mark.   180

GLO'STER   Alack, alack the day!

LEAR   When we are born, we cry that we are come
To this great stage of fools. This a good block.
It were a delicate stratagem to shoe
A troop of horse with felt: I'll put't in proof,
And when I have stol'n upon these son-in-laws,
Then kill, kill, kill, kill, kill, kill!

Enter a GENTLEMAN *with* ATTENDANTS.

GENT.   O, here he is: lay hand upon him. Sir,
Your most dear daughter –

LEAR   No rescue? What, a prisoner? I am even   190
The natural fool of Fortune. Use me well;
You shall have ransom. Let me have surgeons:
I am cut to th'brains.

GENT.   You shall have anything.

LEAR   No seconds? All myself?

	Why, this would make a man a man of salt,
	To use his eyes for garden water-pots,
	Ay, and laying autumn's dust.
GENT.	Good sir –
LEAR	I will die bravely, like a smug bridegroom.[156]
	What! I will be jovial. Come, come:
	I am a king, my masters, know you that? 200
GENT.	You are a royal one, and we obey you.
LEAR	Then there's life in't. Come, an you get it, you shall
	get it by running. Sa, sa, sa, sa.

[*Exeunt Lear, running, and attendants in pursuit.*

GENT.	A sight most pitiful in the meanest wretch,
	Past speaking of in a king! Thou hast a daughter
	Who redeems nature from the general curse
	Which twain have brought her to.[157]
EDGAR	Hail, gentle sir!
GENT.	Sir, speed you. What's your will?
EDGAR	Do you hear aught, sir, of a battle tóward?
GENT.	Most sure, and vulgar: everyone hears that, 210
	Which can distinguish sound.
EDGAR	But, by your favour,
	How near's the other army?
GENT.	Near, and on speedy foot: the main descry
	Stands on the hourly thought.[158]
EDGAR	I thank you, sir: that's all.
GENT.	Though that the Queen on special cause is here,
	Her army is moved on.
EDGAR	I thank you, sir.

[*Exit gentleman.*

GLO'STER	You ever-gentle gods, take my breath from me;
	Let not my worser spirit tempt me again
	To die before you please.
EDGAR	Well pray you, father.
GLO'STER	Now, good sir, what are you? 220
EDGAR	A most poor man, made tame to Fortune's blows,
	Who, by the art of known and feeling sorrows,
	Am pregnant to good pity. Give me your hand;
	I'll lead you to some biding.
GLO'STER	Hearty thanks:

The bounty and the benison of Heaven
To boot, and boot![159]

Enter OSWALD.

OSWALD   A proclaimed prize: most happy!
That eyeless head of thine was first framed flesh
To raise my fortunes. Thou old unhappy traitor,
Briefly thyself remember; the sword is out
That must destroy thee.

GLO'STER   Now let thy friendly hand   230
Put strength enough to't.   [*Edgar interposes.*

OSWALD   Wherefore, bold peasant,
Dar'st thou support a published traitor? Hence,
Lest that th'infection of his fortune take
Like hold on thee. Let go his arm.

EDGAR   Chill not let go, zir, without vurther cagion.[160]

OSWALD   Let go, slave, or thou diest.

EDGAR   Good gentleman, go your gate, and let poor volk pass.
An chud ha' bin zwaggered out of my life, 'twould not
ha' bin zo long as 'tis by a vortnight. Nay, come not
near th'old man; keep out, che vor' ye, or Ice try   240
whither your costard or my ballow be the harder.[161]
Chill be plain with you.

OSWALD   Out, dunghill!

EDGAR   Chill pick your teeth, zir. Come; no matter vor your
foins.[162]   [*They fight. Oswald falls.*

OSWALD   Slave, thou hast slain me. Villain, take my purse;
If ever thou wilt thrive, bury my body,
And give the letters which thou find'st about me
To Edmund, Earl of Gloucester; seek him out
Upon the British party. O, untimely death,   250
Death . . .   [*He dies.*

EDGAR   I know thee well: a serviceable villain,
As duteous to the vices of thy mistress
As badness would desire.

GLO'STER   What, is he dead?

EDGAR   Sit you down, father; rest you.
Let's see these pockets; the letters that he speaks of
May be my friends. He's dead; I am only sorry

He had no other deathsman. Let us see.
Leave, gentle wax; and, manners, blame us not:
To know our enemies' minds we rip their hearts;   260
Their papers is more lawful.[163]
[*He reads:*] 'Let our reciprocal vows be remembered.
You have many opportunities to cut him off: if your
will want not, time and place will be fruitfully offered.
There is nothing done if he return the conqueror: then
am I the prisoner, and his bed my gaol; from the
loathed warmth whereof deliver me, and supply the
place for your labour. Your (wife, so I would say)
affectionate servant, and for you her own for venture.[164]
Goneril.'   270
O indistinguished space of woman's will![165]
A plot upon her virtuous husband's life,
And the exchange my brother! Here in the sands
Thee I'll rake up, thou post unsanctified
Of murderous lechers; and in the mature time
With this ungracious paper strike the sight
Of the death-practised Duke. For him 'tis well
That of thy death and business I can tell.

GLO'STER The King is mad; how stiff is my vild sense
That I stand up and have ingenious feeling   280
Of my huge sorrows! Better I were distract:
So should my thoughts be severed from my griefs,
And woes by wrong imaginations lose
The knowledge of themselves.   [*Drum far off.*

EDGAR   Give me your hand:
Far off methinks I hear the beaten drum.
Come, father, I'll bestow you with a friend.   [*Exeunt.*

SCENE 7.[166]

In the French camp.

Enter CORDELIA, KENT, DOCTOR *and* GENTLEMAN.

CORDELIA O thou good Kent, how shall I live and work
To match thy goodness? My life will be too short,
And every measure fail me.

KENT To be acknowledged, madam, is o'er-paid.
All my reports go with the modest truth;
Nor more, nor clipped, but so.

CORDELIA   Be better suited:
These weeds are memories of those worser hours;
I prithee put them off.

KENT   Pardon, dear madam;
Yet to be known shortens my made intent.
My boon I make it that you know me not   10
Till time, and I, think meet.

CORDELIA Then be't so, my good lord.
 [To the doctor:]   How does the King?

DOCTOR Madam, sleeps still.

CORDELIA O you kind gods,
Cure this great breach in his abusèd nature!
Th'untuned and jarring senses, O wind up,
Of this child-changèd father!

DOCTOR   So please your Majesty
That we may wake the King? He hath slept long.

CORDELIA Be governed by your knowledge, and proceed
I'th'sway of your own will. Is he arrayed?   20

GENT. Ay, madam: in the heaviness of sleep,
We put fresh garments on him.

DOCTOR Be by, good madam, when we do awake him;
I doubt not of his temperance.

CORDELIA   Very well.

   SERVANTS *carry in a chair in which* LEAR,
    royally clad, is sleeping. Soft music.

DOCTOR Please you draw near. – Louder the music there![167]

CORDELIA O my dear father, restoration hang

     Thy medicine on my lips, and let this kiss
     Repair those violent harms that my two sisters
     Have in thy reverence made.
KENT   Kind and dear princess!
CORDELIA Had you not been their father, these white flakes 30
     Did challenge pity of them. Was this a face
     To be opposed against the warring winds,
     To stand against the deep dread-bolted thunder
     In the most terrible and nimble stroke
     Of quick cross-lightning, to watch – poor perdu! –
     With this thin helm?[168] Mine enemy's dog,
     Though he had bit me, should have stood that night
     Against my fire; and wast thou fain (poor father)
     To hovel thee with swine and rogues forlorn,
     In short and musty straw?[169] Alack, alack! 40
     'Tis wonder that thy life and wits at once
     Had not concluded all. – He wakes; speak to him.
DOCTOR Madam, do you; 'tis fittest.
CORDELIA How does my royal lord? How fares your Majesty?
LEAR   You do me wrong to take me out o'th'grave:
     Thou art a soul in bliss; but I am bound
     Upon a wheel of fire,[170] that mine own tears
     Do scald like molten lead.
CORDELIA   Sir, do you know me?
LEAR   You are a spirit, I know; where did you die?
CORDELIA Still, still, far wide! 50
DOCTOR He's scarce awake; let him alone awhile.
LEAR   Where have I been? Where am I? Fair daylight?
     I am mightily abused; I should e'en die with pity
     To see another thus. I know not what to say.
     I will not swear these are my hands; let's see:
     I feel this pin prick. Would I were assured
     Of my condition!
CORDELIA [*kneeling:*]   O, look upon me, sir,
     And hold your hand in benediction o'er me;
     No, sir, you must not kneel.
LEAR   Pray do not mock me;
     I am a very foolish fond old man, 60
     Fourscore and upward, not an hour more nor less;

And, to deal plainly,
I fear I am not in my perfect mind.
Methinks I should know you, and know this man,
Yet I am doubtful: for I am mainly ignorant
What place this is; and all the skill I have
Remembers not these garments, nor I know not
Where I did lodge last night. Do not laugh at me,
For (as I am a man) I think this lady
To be my child Cordelia.

CORDELIA   And so I am: I am!   70

LEAR   Be your tears wet? Yes, faith: I pray weep not.
If you have poison for me, I will drink it:
I know you do not love me, for your sisters
Have (as I do remember) done me wrong;
You have some cause; they have not.

CORDELIA   No cause, no cause.

LEAR   Am I in France?

KENT   In your own kingdom, sir.

LEAR   Do not abuse me.

DOCTOR   Be comforted, good madam: the great rage,
You see, is killed in him; and yet it is danger
To make him even o'er the time he has lost.   80
Desire him to go in; trouble him no more
Till further settling.[171]

CORDELIA   Will't please your Highness walk?

LEAR   You must bear with me. Pray you now, forget and forgive;
I am old and foolish. [*Exeunt all but Kent and gentleman.*

GENT.   Holds it true, sir, that the Duke of Cornwall was so slain?

KENT   Most certain, sir.

GENT.   Who is conductor of his people?

KENT   As 'tis said, the bastard son of Gloucester.

GENT.   They say Edgar, his banished son, is with the Earl of 90
Kent in Germany.

KENT   Report is changeable. 'Tis time to look about; the
powers of the kingdom approach apace.

GENT.   The arbitrement is like to be bloody. Fare you well, sir.
                                           [*Exit.*

KENT   My point and period will be throughly wrought,
Or well or ill, as this day's battle's fought.[172]   [*Exit.*

ACT 5, SCENE 1.

The British camp near Dover.

Enter, with drum and colours, EDMUND, REGAN,
*   GENTLEMEN and* SOLDIERS.

EDMUND   Know of the Duke if his last purpose hold,
           Or whether since he is advised by aught
           To change the course. He's full of alteration
           And self-reproving; bring his constant pleasure.
                                        [*Exit gentleman.*
REGAN   Our sister's man is certainly miscarried.
EDMUND   'Tis to be doubted, madam.
REGAN   Now, sweet lord,
           You know the goodness I intend upon you.
           Tell me but truly – but then speak the truth[173] –
           Do you not love my sister?
EDMUND   In honoured love.
REGAN   But have you never found my brother's way   10
           To the forfended place?
EDMUND   That thought abuses you.
REGAN   I am doubtful that you have been conjunct
           And bosomed with her, as far as we call hers.[174]
EDMUND   No, by mine honour, madam.
REGAN   I never shall endure her. Dear my lord,
           Be not familiar with her.
EDMUND   Fear me not.
           She and the Duke her husband!

Enter, with drum and colours, ALBANY, GONERIL *and* SOLDIERS.

GONERIL   [*aside:*] I had rather lose the battle than that sister
           Should loosen him and me.[175]
ALBANY   Our very loving sister, well be-met.   20
           – Sir, this I hear: the King is come to his daughter,
           With others whom the rigour of our state
           Forced to cry out. Where I could not be honest,
           I never yet was valiant: for this business,
           It touches us as France invades our land,
           Not bolds the King, with others whom, I fear,

Most just and heavy causes make oppose.

EDMUND   Sir, you speak nobly.[176]

REGAN   Why is this reasoned?

GONERIL   Combine together 'gainst the enemy;
For these domestic and particular broils   30
Are not the question here.

ALBANY   Let's then determine
With th'ancient of war on our proceeding.

EDMUND   I shall attend you presently at your tent.

REGAN   Sister, you'll go with us?

GONERIL   No.

REGAN   Tis most convenient; pray go with us.

GONERIL   O ho, I know the riddle.[177] – I will go.

As they are going out, enter EDGAR *disguised.*

EDGAR   If e'er your Grace had speech with man so poor,
Hear me one word.

ALBANY   [*to those leaving:*]   I'll overtake you.
                [*Exeunt all but Albany and Edgar.*
                    Speak.

EDGAR   Before you fight the battle, ope this letter.   40
If you have victory, let the trumpet sound
For him that brought it. Wretched though I seem,
I can produce a champion that will prove
What is avouchèd there. If you miscarry,
Your business of the world hath so an end,
And machination ceases. Fortune love you!

ALBANY   Stay till I have read the letter.

EDGAR   I was forbid it.
When time shall serve, let but the herald cry,
And I'll appear again.

ALBANY   Why, fare thee well;
I will o'erlook thy paper.   [*Exit Edgar.* 50

Enter EDMUND.

EDMUND   The enemy's in view; draw up your powers.
Here is the guess of their true strength and forces,
By diligent discovery; but your haste
Is now urged on you.

ALBANY   We will greet the time.   [*Exit.*

EDMUND   To both these sisters have I sworn my love;
         Each jealous of the other, as the stung
         Are of the adder. Which of them shall I take?
         Both? One? Or neither? Neither can be enjoyed
         If both remain alive: to take the widow
         Exasperates, makes mad her sister Goneril;   · 60
         And hardly shall I carry out my side,
         Her husband being alive. Now then, we'll use
         His countenance for the battle, which being done,
         Let her who would be rid of him devise
         His speedy taking off. As for the mercy
         Which he intends to Lear and to Cordelia:
         The battle done, and they within our power,
         Shall never see his pardon: for my state
         Stands on me to defend, not to debate.   [*Exit.*

SCENE 2.

A field between the two camps.

Alarum heard. Enter, with drum and colours, CORDELIA, *leading* LEAR
      by the hand, and French SOLDIERS. *Exeunt.*[178]

Enter EDGAR *and* GLOUCESTER.

EDGAR   Here, father, take the shadow of this tree
         For your good host. Pray that the right may thrive.
         If ever I return to you again,
         I'll bring you comfort.
GLO'STER   Grace go with you, sir! [*Exit Edgar.*

Alarum heard from the battlefield, and later a retreat.

Enter EDGAR.

EDGAR   Away, old man; give me thy hand, away!
         King Lear hath lost, he and his daughter ta'en.
         Give me thy hand; come on!
GLO'STER No further, sir; a man may rot even here.
EDGAR   What, in ill thoughts again? Men must endure
         Their going hence, even as their coming hither;   10
         Ripeness is all.[179] Come on.
GLO'STER   And that's true too. [*Exeunt.*

SCENE 3.

The British camp near Dover.

Enter: in conquest with drum and colours, EDMUND; LEAR *and*
CORDELIA as prisoners; CAPTAIN *and* SOLDIERS.

EDMUND　　Some officers take them away: good guard,
　　　　　Until their greater pleasures first be known
　　　　　That are to censure them.

CORDELIA　[*to Lear:*]　　　　　　We are not the first
　　　　　Who with best meaning have incurred the worst.
　　　　　For thee, oppressèd King, I am cast down;
　　　　　Myself could else out-frown false Fortune's frown.
　　　　　Shall we not see these daughters and these sisters?

LEAR　　　No, no, no, no! Come, let's away to prison:
　　　　　We two alone will sing like birds i'th'cage;
　　　　　When thou dost ask me blessing, I'll kneel down　　　10
　　　　　And ask of thee forgiveness. So we'll live,
　　　　　And pray, and sing, and tell old tales, and laugh
　　　　　At gilded butterflies, and hear poor rogues
　　　　　Talk of court news; and we'll talk with them too –
　　　　　Who loses and who wins, who's in, who's out –
　　　　　And take upon's the mystery of things,
　　　　　As if we were God's spies; and we'll wear out,
　　　　　In a walled prison, packs and sects of great ones
　　　　　That ebb and flow by th'moon.[180]

EDMUND　　　　　　　　　　　　　　Take them away.

LEAR　　　Upon such sacrifices, my Cordelia,　　　　　　20
　　　　　The gods themselves throw incense. Have I caught thee?
　　　　　He that parts us shall bring a brand from heaven
　　　　　And fire us hence like foxes.[181] Wipe thine eyes;
　　　　　The good years shall devour them, flesh and fell,
　　　　　Ere they shall make us weep! We'll see 'em starved first.
　　　　　Come.　　　　　　　　　[*Exeunt Lear and Cordelia, guarded.*

EDMUND　　Come hither, captain; hark.
　　　　　Take thou this note.
　　　　　[*He gives a paper.*]　　Go follow them to prison.
　　　　　One step I have advanced thee; if thou dost

As this instructs thee, thou dost make thy way   30
To noble fortunes. Know thou this, that men
Are as the time is; to be tender-minded
Does not become a sword. Thy great employment
Will not bear question: either say thou'lt do't,
Or thrive by other means.

CAPTAIN   I'll do't, my lord.

EDMUND   About it; and write 'happy' when th'hast done.
Mark – I say instantly; and carry it so
As I have set it down.

CAPTAIN   I cannot draw a cart, nor eat dried oats;
If it be man's work I'll do't.[182]
                                            [*Exit.* 40

Flourish. Enter ALBANY, GONERIL, REGAN *and* SOLDIERS.

ALBANY   Sir, you have showed today your valiant strain,
And Fortune led you well. You have the captives
Who were the opposites of this day's strife:
I do require them of you, so to use them
As we shall find their merits and our safety
May equally determine.

EDMUND   Sir, I thought it fit
To send the old and miserable King
To some retention and appointed guard;
Whose age had charms in it, whose title more,
To pluck the common bosom on his side,   50
And turn our impressed lances in our eyes
Which do command them. With him I sent the Queen,
My reason all the same; and they are ready
Tomorrow, or at further space, t'appear
Where you shall hold your session. At this time
We sweat and bleed: the friend hath lost his friend;
And the best quarrels, in the heat, are cursed
By those that feel their sharpness.
The question of Cordelia and her father
Requires a fitter place.[183]

ALBANY   Sir, by your patience,   60
I hold you but a subject of this war,
Not as a brother.

REGAN   That's as we list to grace him.

Methinks our pleasure might have been demanded
Ere you had spoke so far. He led our powers,
Bore the commission of my place and person,
The which immediacy may well stand up
And call itself your brother.

GONERIL   Not so hot!
In his own grace he doth exalt himself
More than in your addition.

REGAN   In my rights
By me invested, he compeers the best.   70

ALBANY   That were the most if he should husband you.[184]

REGAN   Jesters do oft prove prophets.

GONERIL   Hóla, hóla!
That eye that told you so looked but asquint.

REGAN   Lady, I am not well, else I should answer
From a full-flowing stomach. [*To Edmund:*] General,
Take thou my soldiers, prisoners, patrimony:
Dispose of them, of me; the walls are thine.[185]
Witness the world that I create thee here
My lord and master.

GONERIL   Mean you to enjoy him?

ALBANY   The let-alone lies not in your good will.[186]   80

EDMUND   Nor in thine, lord.

ALBANY   Half-blooded fellow, yes.

REGAN   [*to Edmund:*]
Let the drum strike; and prove my title thine.[187]

ALBANY   Stay yet; hear reason. Edmund, I arrest thee
On capital treason, and, in thy attaint,
[*indicating Goneril:*]
This gilded serpent. [*To Regan:*] For your claim,
                            fair sister,
I bar it in the interest of my wife:
'Tis she is sub-contracted to this lord,
And I, her husband, contradict your banns.
If you will marry, make your loves to me;
My lady is bespoke.

GONERIL   An interlude!   90

ALBANY   Thou art armed, Gloucester: let the trumpet sound.
If none appear to prove upon thy person

Thy heinous, manifest, and many treasons,
There is my pledge.   [*He throws down his gauntlet.*
                              I'll make it on thy heart,
Ere I taste bread, thou art in nothing less
Than I have here proclaimed thee.

REGAN   Sick, O sick!

GONERIL   [*aside:*] If not, I'll ne'er trust medicine.

EDMUND   There's my exchange!   [*He throws down his gauntlet.*
                              What in the world he is
That names me traitor, villain-like he lies.
Call by the trumpet; he that dares approach,   100
On him, on you – who not? – I will maintain
My truth and honour firmly.

ALBANY   A herald, ho!

EDMUND   A herald, ho, a herald!

ALBANY   Trust to thy single virtue; for the soldiers,
All levied in my name, have in my name
Took their discharge.

REGAN   My sickness grows upon me.

ALBANY   She is not well; convey her to my tent.
                                        [*Exit Regan, aided.*

                    Enter a HERALD.

Come hither, herald – Let the trumpet sound –
And read out this.   [*A trumpet sounds.*

HERALD   [*reads:*] 'If any man of quality or degree within the lists   110
of the army will maintain upon Edmund, supposed
Earl of Gloucester, that he is a manifold traitor, let him
appear by the third sound of the trumpet. He is bold in
his defence.'   [*First trumpet-call.*
Again!   [*Second trumpet-call.*
Again!   [*Third trumpet-call.*

        An answering trumpet is heard. Enter EDGAR, *in armour.*

ALBANY   Ask him his purposes – why he appears
Upon this call o'th'trumpet.

HERALD   What are you?
Your name, your quality, and why you answer
This present summons?

EDGAR   Know my name is lost,   120

By treason's tooth bare-gnawn and canker-bit;
Yet am I noble as the adversary
I come to cope.

ALBANY   Which is that adversary?

EDGAR   What's he that speaks for Edmund, Earl of Gloucester?

EDMUND   Himself; what say'st thou to him?

EDGAR   Draw thy sword,
That, if my speech offend a noble heart,
Thy arm may do thee justice; here is mine:
Behold, it is the privilege of mine honours,
My oath, and my profession. I protest,
Maugre thy strength, place, youth and eminence,   130
Despite thy victor-sword and fire-new fortune,
Thy valour and thy heart, thou art a traitor,
False to thy gods, thy brother and thy father,
Conspirant 'gainst this high illustrious prince,
And, from th'extremest upward of thy head
To the descent and dust below thy foot,
A most toad-spotted traitor. Say thou 'No',
This sword, this arm and my best spirits are bent
To prove upon thy heart, whereto I speak,
Thou liest.

EDMUND   In wisdom I should ask thy name;   140
But since thy outside looks so fair and warlike,
And that thy tongue some say of breeding breathes,
What safe and nicely I might well delay[188]
By rule of knighthood, I disdain and spurn.
Back do I toss these treasons to thy head,
With the hell-hated lie o'erwhelm thy heart,
Which, for they yet glance by and scarcely bruise,
This sword of mine shall give them instant way
Where they shall rest for ever.[189] Trumpets, speak!

Alarums. They fight. Edmund falls.

ALBANY   Save him, save him!

GONERIL   This is practice, Gloucester: 150
By th'law of war thou wast not bound to answer
An unknown opposite. Thou art not vanquished,
But cozened and beguiled.

ALBANY   Shut your mouth, dame,

Or with this paper shall I stop it.
[*To Edmund:*]   Hold, sir:
Thou worse than any name, read thine own evil.
[*To Goneril:*] No tearing, lady! I perceive you know it.

GONERIL Say if I do – the laws are mine,[190] not thine;
Who can arraign me for't?   [*Exit.*[191]

ALBANY   Most monstrous! O!
[*To Edmund:*] Know'st thou this paper?

EDMUND   Ask me not what I know.

ALBANY [*to a soldier:*] Go after her: she's desperate; govern her.   160
                                         [*Exit soldier.*

EDMUND What you have charged me with, that have I done,
And more, much more; the time will bring it out.
'Tis past, and so am I. [*To Edgar:*] But what art thou
That hast this fortune on me? If thou'rt noble,
I do forgive thee.

EDGAR   Let's exchange charity.
I am no less in blood than thou art, Edmund;
If more, the more th'hast wronged me.
My name is Edgar, and thy father's son.
The gods are just, and of our pleasant vices
Make instruments to plague us: 170
The dark and vicious place where thee he got
Cost him his eyes.

EDMUND   Thou'st spoken right, 'tis true.
The wheel is come full circle; I am here.

ALBANY [*to Edgar:*] Methought thy very gait did prophesy
A royal nobleness. I must embrace thee.
Let sorrow split my heart if ever I
Did hate thee or thy father.

EDGAR   Worthy prince, I know't.

ALBANY Where have you hid yourself?
How have you known the miseries of your father?

EDGAR By nursing them, my lord. List a brief tale;   180
And when 'tis told, O that my heart would burst!
The bloody proclamation to escape
That followed me so near (O, our life's sweetness!
That we the pain of death would hourly die,
Rather than die at once!) taught me to shift

Into a madman's rags, t'assume a semblance
That very dogs disdained; and in this habit
Met I my father with his bleeding rings,
Their precious stones new lost; became his guide,
Led him, begged for him, saved him from despair;   190
Never (O fault!) revealed myself unto him
Until some half-hour past, when I was armed.
Not sure, though hoping, of this good success,
I asked his blessing, and from first to last
Told him our pilgrimage. But his flawed heart
(Alack, too weak the conflict to support!)
'Twixt two extremes of passion, joy and grief,
Burst smilingly.

EDGAR   This speech of yours hath moved me,
And shall perchance do good; but speak you on:
You look as you had something more to say.   200

ALBANY If there be more, more woeful, hold it in,
For I am almost ready to dissolve,
Hearing of this.

EDGAR   This would have seemed a period
To such as love not sorrow; but another,
To amplify too much, would make much more,
And top extremity.[192] Whilst I
Was big in clamour, came there in a man,
Who, having seen me in my worst estate,
Shunned my abhorred society; but then, finding
Who 'twas that so endured, with his strong arms   210
He fastened on my neck and bellowed out
As he'd burst heaven; threw him on my father;
Told the most piteous tale of Lear and him
That ever ear received, which in recounting,
His grief grew puissant and the strings of life
Began to crack. Twice then the trumpets sounded,
And there I left him tranced.

ALBANY   But who was this?

EDGAR Kent, sir, the banished Kent, who in disguise
Followed his enemy King and did him service
Improper for a slave.[193]   220

Enter a GENTLEMAN *with a blood-stained knife.*

GENT.	Help, help! O help!
EDGAR	What kind of help?
ALBANY	Speak, man!
EDGAR	What means this bloody knife?
GENT.	'Tis hot, it smokes;

It came even from the heart of – O, she's dead!

ALBANY Who dead? Speak, man!

GENT. Your lady, sir, your lady; and her sister
By her is poisoned: she confesses it.

EDMUND I was contracted to them both; all three
Now marry in an instant.

EDGAR   Here comes Kent.

Enter KENT.

ALBANY Produce the bodies, be they alive or dead.
                              [*Exit gentleman.*
This judgement of the heavens, that makes us tremble, 230
Touches us not with pity. [*He sees Kent:*] O, is this he?
[*To Kent:*] The time will not allow the compliment
Which very manners urges.

KENT   I am come
To bid my King and master aye good night.
Is he not here?

ALBANY   Great thing of us forgot!
Speak, Edmund: where's the King? And where's
                                        Cordelia?
            [*The bodies of Goneril and Regan are brought on.*
See'st thou this object, Kent?

KENT   Alack, why thus?

EDMUND Yet Edmund was beloved:
The one the other poisoned for my sake,
And after slew herself.   240

ALBANY Even so. Cover their faces.

EDMUND I pant for life. Some good I mean to do,
Despite of mine own nature. Quickly send
(Be brief in it) to th'castle, for my writ
Is on the life of Lear and on Cordelia.
Nay, send in time!

ALBANY   Run, run, O run!

EDGAR	To who, my lord? [*To Edmund:*] Who has the office?
	<div align="right">Send</div>
	Thy token of reprieve.
EDMUND	Well thought on. Take my sword; the captain –
	Give it the captain.
EDGAR	[*to gentleman:*] Haste thee, for thy life!¹⁹⁴

[Exit gentleman.]

EDMUND   [*to Albany:*] He hath commission from thy wife and me
To hang Cordelia in the prison, and
To lay the blame upon her own despair,
That she fordid herself.

ALBANY   The gods defend her!
Bear him hence awhile.   [*Edmund is carried off.*

Enter LEAR *with* CORDELIA *in his arms.* GENTLEMAN *follows.*

LEAR   Howl, howl, howl! O, you are men of stones!
Had I your tongues and eyes, I'd use them so
That heaven's vault should crack! She's gone for ever.
[*He lays her down:*]
I know when one is dead, and when one lives;
She's dead as earth. Lend me a looking-glass:
If that her breath will mist or stain the stone,
Why then she lives.

KENT   Is this the promised end?¹⁹⁵

EDGAR   Or image of that horror?

ALBANY   Fall and cease!¹⁹⁶

LEAR   This feather stirs, she lives: if it be so,¹⁹⁷
It is a chance which does redeem all sorrows
That ever I have felt.

KENT   O my good master!

LEAR   Prithee away!

EDGAR   'Tis noble Kent, your friend.

LEAR   A plague upon you, murderers, traitors all!
I might have saved her; now she's gone for ever. –
Cordelia, Cordelia, stay a little. Ha?
What is't thou say'st? – Her voice was ever soft,
Gentle and low, an excellent thing in woman. –
I killed the slave that was a-hanging thee.

GENT.   'Tis true, my lords, he did.

LEAR   Did I not, fellow?

250

260

270

I have seen the day, with my good biting falchion
I would have made them skip; I am old now,
And these same crosses spoil me. Who are you?
Mine eyes are not o'th'best, I'll tell you straight.

KENT   If Fortune brag of two she loved and hated,
One of them we behold.   280

LEAR   This is a dull sight.[198] – Are you not Kent?

KENT   The same:
Your servant Kent. Where is your servant Caius?

LEAR   He's a good fellow, I can tell you that;
He'll strike, and quickly too. He's dead and rotten.

KENT   No, my good lord; I am the very man –

LEAR   I'll see that straight.

KENT   That from your first of difference and decay
Have followed your sad steps –

LEAR   You're welcome hither.

KENT   Nor no man else. All's cheerless, dark, and deadly.
Your eldest daughters have fordone themselves,   290
And desperately are dead.

LEAR   Ay, so I think.

ALBANY   He knows not what he says, and vain is it
That we present us to him.

EDGAR   Very bootless.

Enter a MESSENGER.

MESSENGER Edmund is dead, my lord.

ALBANY   That's but a trifle here.
You lords and noble friends, know our intent:
What comfort to this great decay may come
Shall be applied. For us, we will resign,
During the life of this old Majesty,
To him our absolute power;
[*to Edgar and Kent:*]   you, to your rights,
With boot and such addition as your honours   300
Have more than merited. All friends shall taste
The wages of their virtue, and all foes
The cup of their deservings. – O see, see!

LEAR   And my poor fool is hanged![199] No, no, no life!
Why should a dog, a horse, a rat have life,

And thou no breath at all? Thou'lt come no more,
Never, never, never, never, never!
– Pray you, undo this button. Thank you, sir.
Do you see this? Look on her! Look, her lips,
Look there, look there!   [*Lear dies.*[200]

EDGAR   He faints. – My lord, my lord!   310

KENT   Break, heart; I prithee break.

EDGAR   Look up, my lord.

KENT   Vex not his ghost: O let him pass; he hates him,
That would upon the rack of this tough world
Stretch him out longer.

EDGAR   He is gone indeed.

KENT   The wonder is he hath endured so long;
He but usurped his life.

ALBANY   Bear them from hence. Our present business
Is general woe.
[*To Kent and Edgar:*] Friends of my soul, you twain,
Rule in this realm, and the gored state sustain.[201]

KENT   I have a journey, sir, shortly to go: 320
My master calls me; I must not say no.

EDGAR   The weight of this sad time we must obey;
Speak what we feel, not what we ought to say.
The oldest hath borne most; we that are young
Shall never see so much, nor live so long.[202]

                              [*Exeunt with a dead march.*

NOTES ON *KING LEAR*

In these notes, the abbreviations used include the following:

F1:   First Folio (1623);

Harsnett: Samuel Harsnett: *A Declaration of Egregious Popish Impostures* (London: Roberts, 1603);

i.e.:   *id est*: that is;

O.E.D.: *The Oxford English Dictionary* (2nd edition, 1989, and website);

Q1:   First Quarto (1607–8);

Q1c: First Quarto, as corrected during printing;

Q1u: First Quarto, uncorrected;

RF: *King Lear*, ed. R. A. Foakes (Walton-on-Thames: Nelson, 1997);

S.D.:   stage direction.

Biblical quotations are from the Geneva Bible (1560).

In the case of a pun or an ambiguity, the meanings are distinguished as (a) and (b), or as (a), (b) and (c).

1 (1.1.5–6) *qualities . . . moiety*: 'their qualities are so equally balanced that after a careful scrutiny it is impossible to prefer one share to the other'.

2 (1.1.34) Exit.: F1 has this S.D., though Q1 has no direction here. Some editors specify that Edmund leaves with Gloucester, as Q1 and F1 provide no subsequent exit for Edmund.

3 (1.1.39–44) *while we . . . now*: This passage is present in the Folio text but absent from the Quarto.

4 (1.1.48–9) *(Since . . . state)*: These lines are present in F1 but absent from Q1.

5 (1.1.52) *where nature doth with merit challenge*: 'where merit, as
   well as birthright, makes the claim'.

6 (1.1.63–4) *champains . . . meads*: The champains (open plains)
   and plenteous rivers are mentioned in F1 but not in Q1.

7 (1.1.82–4) *Although . . . interessed*: Q1 has: 'Although the last, not
   least in our deere loue'; F1 has: 'Although our last and least; to
   whose yong loue, / The Vines of France, and Milke of Burgundie,
   / Striue to be interest'. (Here, 'be interest' means 'lay claim'.)

8 (1.1.89) *Nothing will come of nothing*: a proverbial version of the
   Aristotelian maxim, 'Ex nihilo nihil fit': 'Nothing is made from
   nothing'.

9 (1.1.205) *Election . . . conditions*: 'With those conditions, it is
   impossible to confirm my choice.'

10 (1.1.238–9) *regards . . . point*: 'utterly irrelevant considerations'.

11 (1.1.276–7) *You . . . wanted*: 'You were disobedient, and you
    well deserve as little love from your husband as you have granted
    your father.'

12 (1.1.278–9) *Time . . . derides*: 'Time, who eventually exposes to
    mockery covert faults, will unwrap what cunning wraps up.'

13 (1.1.291) *The best . . . rash*: 'Even in the prime of life, he
    displayed rashness'.

14 (1.1.299–301) *If . . . us*: 'If our father continues to wield
    authority in his habitual manner, this recent concession of his
    will only harm us.'

15 (1.2.1) *Thou . . . goddess*: because he is a 'natural' (illegitimate)
    son. By 'Nature' he means (in part) 'the natural as opposed to the
    conventional': the bestial and appetitive, as opposed to traditional
    law and order.

16 (1.2.3) *in . . . custom*: 'plagued by convention'.

17 (1.2.21) *top th'legitimate*: 'surpass the legitimate brother'. An
    editorial emendation, 'top', replaces Q1's 'too' and F1's 'to''.

18 (1.2.91–3) *Nor . . . earth!*: This piece of dialogue is present in
    Q1 but absent from F1.

19 (1.2.95–6) *unstate . . . resolution*: 'gladly lose my rank and wealth
    to be freed from my uncertainty'.

20 (1.2.105–110) *This . . . graves*: This passage is absent from Q1
    but present in F1.

21 (1.2.126) *Fut!*: (a) version of French *foutre*: 'Fuck!'; (b) 'By

God's [or Christ's] foot!'. This exclamation is present in Q1 but absent (probably because of censorship) from F1.

22 (1.2.129) *Pat . . . comedy*: 'How neat: he arrives with implausibly convenient timing, like the dénouement of an old-fashioned comic interlude.'

23 (1.2.131) *Tom o'Bedlam*: beggar who supposedly came from Bedlam (the hospital of St Mary of Bethlehem in London, incorporated in 1547 as a home for the insane). Where Q1 has 'sith like them of Bedlam'; F1 has 'sighe like *Tom* o'Bedlam'.

24 (1.2.132) *divisions . . . me*: 'Divisions' could mean not only 'discords' but also 'musical variations on a theme'. Edmund proceeds (in F1, not Q1) to sing four notes from the musical scale.

25 (1.2.138–45) *unhappily . . . astronomical?*: This passage is in Q1. F1 has 'vnhappily.' and lacks the rest of the passage. A 'sectary astronomical' is a devotee of astrology.

26 (1.2.159–64) *I pray . . . brother?*: This passage is absent from Q1 but present in F1.

27 (1.3.16–21) *one . . . abused*: This passage is present in Q1. F1 has 'one, / Remember what I haue said.', and omits the remainder. Line 21 means 'with rebukes instead of flattery, when they are seen to be deluded'.

28 (1.3.25–6) *I would . . . speak*: 'I wish to generate from this basis pretexts for speaking my mind, and I will.' This sentence is present in Q1 but absent from F1.

29 (1.4. S.D. after 7) Horns . . . ATTENDANTS.: Q1 has simply '*Enter Lear.*', and in speech-prefixes refers to the attendants as servants. F1 has '*Hornes within. Enter Lear and Attendants.*', and in speech-prefixes refers to the attendants as knights.

30 (1.4.16) *eat no fish*: He may mean (a) that he is a full-blooded person (a meat-eater), or (b) that he insists on a good diet, or (c, anachronistically) that he is no Catholic (as Catholics eat fish on Fridays).

31 (1.4.80) *football player*: an insult, football being deemed (in Shakespeare's day) a vulgar amusement.

32 (1.4.93–4) *an . . . shortly*: 'if you cannot ingratiate yourself with those who are gaining power, you will find yourself out in the cold'.

33 (1.4.109–18) *Have . . . score*: The glossary explains the details, but the gist of these rhyming couplets is: 'Behave prudently and you'll make money'.

34 (1.4.130–45) *That lord . . . snatching*: These lines are present in
Q1 but absent from F1.

35 (1.4.155–8) *Fools . . . apish*: The gist is that fools are no longer
needed because wise men have become stupid.

36 (1.4.180–81) *an O . . . figure*: 'a zero without another digit
before it'.

37 (1.4.185–6) *He . . . some*: 'He who gives everything away
because he's tired of it will later be in need.'

38 (1.4.196–201) *which . . . proceeding*: 'If you do this, I will criticise
you and seek redress. My actions, intended to maintain a healthy
system, may offend you. To cause such offence would be
shameful if it were not so necessary, and thus to be regarded as
prudent policy.'

39 (1.4.212) *Whoop . . . thee*: This may be the refrain of a song.
'Jug' could be (a) a nickname for 'Joan', or (b) slang for
'maidservant', 'sweetheart' or 'sexual partner', or (c) a direct
reference to a jug of ale.

40 (1.4.218–21) *Lear's . . . father*: Q1 allocates '*Lears* shadow?' to
Lear; F1 allocates '*Lears* shadow.' to the Fool. F1 lacks the
remainder of this passage.

41 (1.4.223–4) *This . . . pranks*: 'This feigned wonderment is very
similar to your other new eccenticities.'

42 (1.4.253) *O most small fault*: probably reluctance to be elo-
quently dutiful.

43 (1.4.255–6) *Which . . . place*: 'which, like an implement,
wrenched my natural disposition from its point of reference'.

44 (1.4.309–20) *This . . . th'unfitness*: These lines are absent from
Q1 but present in F1.

45 (1.5.7–11) *If . . . ha!*: Lear agrees with the Fool that a man's
brains, if they were in his heels, might suffer from chilblains. The
Fool replies that there is no need for Lear to wear slippers (to
make chilblains less sore). He implies that Lear has no brains even
in his feet, for, if he had some, he would not proceed hopefully
to Regan.

46 (1.5.45–6) *She . . . shorter*: These words are addressed by the
Fool to women in the audience. He probably means: 'Any virgin
present who laughs as I go offstage will not remain a virgin long –
unless penises are docked.'

47 (2.1.82–4) *of my land . . . capable*: 'I'll rewrite my will so that
you, loyal and filial boy, inherit my estate instead of Edgar'.

48 (2.1.110–11) *Make . . . please*: 'When effecting your plan, use my authority and resources as you wish.'

49 (2.2.8) *in Lipsbury Pinfold*: perhaps 'penned within my lips', i.e. 'between my teeth'.

50 (2.2.17–18) *one . . . service*: 'a person whose idea of good service includes pimping'.

51 (2.2.29–30) *I'll . . . barber-monger*: 'I'll make you into a bit of sodden toast, so perforated that the moonlight will soak into you and shine through you, you bastard, you base fop.' ('Sop o'th'moonshine' puzzles commentators, and this interpretation of it is speculative.)

52 (2.2.33–4) *take . . . father*: 'against the majesty of Lear take sides with Goneril, who resembles the personification of female vanity in a morality-play performed in puppet-shows'.

53 (2.2.73–4) *turn . . . masters*: The halcyon (kingfisher), when dead and suspended, was supposed to turn its beak in accordance with changes in the wind. Kent says that sycophantic servants likewise reflect and support every changeable mood of their masters.

54 (2.2.78–9) *Goose . . . Camelot*: 'If I found you on Salisbury Plain, you would cackle in fear as I drove you all the way to King Arthur's legendary castle, you silly goose.'

55 (2.2.103) *Phoebus' front*: the forehead of Phoebus Apollo, the sun-god.

56 (2.2.107–8) *though . . . to't*: 'even though, if you begged me to be a plain-spoken rogue and I refused, you would be annoyed'.

57 (2.2.119–20) *None . . . Fool*: 'Any of these rogues and cowards can make a Fool of Ajax.' (The legendary Greek warrior, Ajax, was brave but stupid. The implication is that the powerful Cornwall is stupid enough to be fooled even by Oswald.)

58 (2.2.135–9) *His fault . . . with*: This passage is present in Q1 but absent from F1.

59 (2.2.145) *Come, my good lord, away*: Q1 ascribes to Regan the words 'Come my good Lord away?'. F1, instead, ascribes to Cornwall the words 'Come my Lord, away.' The speech is more appropriate as an injunction from Regan to Cornwall (who departs with her) than from Cornwall to Gloucester (who remains).

60 (2.2.155–6) *Thou . . . sun*: 'You go from heaven's blessing to the sun's heat': from good to bad.

61 (2.2.157) *beacon . . . globe*: moon (illuminator of this world beneath it).

62 (2.2.159–60) *Nothing . . . misery*: 'When we are in the depths of misery, any relief seems miraculous.'

63 (2.2.163) *From . . . state*: 'from this monstrous state of affairs'. (A line of Shakespeare may be missing before this phrase.)

64 (2.2.167) *wheel*: It was said that the goddess Fortune turned a wheel, and, as she did so, a person's luck would change.

65 (2.3.14) *Bedlam beggars*: another reference to the beggars or vagabonds who purported to be from Bethlehem Hospital. John Awdeley's *The Fraternitye of Vacabondes* (1561) and Thomas Dekker's *The Belman of London* (1608) claim that such beggars used the name 'Poor Tom' and stuck pins in their flesh.

66 (2.3.20) *Turlygod*: perhaps 'whining beggar', from Gaelic; but editors are generally baffled by this name.

67 (2.4. heading) SCENE 4: In Q1 and F1 this scene is not separated from the previous one, but editors have frequently separated it. The action is continuous.

68 (2.4.7, 9–10) *cruel, When . . . legs*: The adjective 'cruel' puns on 'crewel', meaning 'thin worsted yarn'. 'When a man's over-lusty at legs' means (a) 'When a man runs away (from his master)', and (b) 'When a man is sexually over-active'.

69 (2.4.18–19) *No . . . have*: These words are present in Q1 but absent from F1. Kent's words in line 21 are only in F1.

70 (2.4.45–53) *Winter's . . . year*: This passage is absent from Q1 but present in F1. Line 45 is a warning that more trouble is brewing. (Wild geese were supposed to take wing noisily when bad weather approached.) In line 47, 'blind' means 'blind to their fathers' needs'; the 'bags' of 48 are money-bags. Line 51 means 'never opens the door to the needy'. In 52, 'dolours' means griefs and is a pun on 'dollars'.

71 (2.4.54–5) *this mother . . . Hysterica passio*: 'Mother' was another name of *hysterica passio* ('suffering in the womb'), giddiness supposedly caused by 'wind in the bottom of the belly'.

72 (2.4.65–8) *We'll set . . . stinking*: Aesop, in his *Fables*, says that the provident ant labours in the summer to gather stores for the winter. Proverbs 6:6–8 urges the sluggard to learn prudence from the ant. The Fool means that Kent is industrious on Lear's behalf at the wrong season (when Lear is out of favour), and that even a

blind man can discern that Lear is now no better than rotting carrion.

73 (2.4.80–81) *The knave . . . perdy*:   Apparently contradicting what the Fool has just recited, these lines seem to declare that the rogue who runs away thereby becomes a fool, whereas the Fool himself is no rogue. Dr Johnson suggested that line 80 should begin: 'The fool turns knave'. In that line, however, 'knave' could mean merely 'servant' or 'lad', in contrast to its meaning ('rogue') in line 81. 'Perdy', from the French *par Dieu*, means 'by God'.

74 (2.4.93–4) *Well . . . man?*:   These words are absent from Q1 but present in F1, as are the words from 'Are' to '"Fiery"? The' at 98–9.

75 (2.4.97) *commands her service*:   Q1 has, in uncorrected issues, 'come and tends seruise'; in corrected issues, 'commands her seruice'. F1 has 'commands, tends, seruise'. RF reads 'commands – tends – service', meaning 'commands – on second thoughts awaits – her service'.

76 (2.4.101–2) *Infirmity . . . bound*:   'When we are ill, we always neglect the duties that we are bound to undertake when we are well.'

77 (2.4.104–7) *I'll . . . man*:   'I'll be patient, and I now oppose my more headstong tendency to mistake the spell of indisposition and sickness for (pretences by) a healthy man.'

78 (2.4.114) *cry sleep to death*:   'summon sleep to execution'.

79 (2.4.117–21) *Cry . . . hay*:   A 'cockney' is a foolishly affected woman. The point here is that both the cockney and her brother (like Lear in the past with Regan and Goneril) have been stupidly kind but with cruel results. She cannot bring herself to kill the eels before baking them in a pie, but then tries to beat them down when they seek to escape from it. (Lear's attempt to repel his grief will be as futile.) Her brother well meaningly butters the horse's hay, but thus makes it greasily inedible.

80 (2.4.135–40) *Say . . . blame*:   These lines are absent from Q1 but present in F1.

81 (2.4.163–4) *To fall . . . mood* –:   'To fall and blast her pride!' follows Q1, but substitutes an exclamation-mark for Q1's full stop; F1 has 'To fall, and blister.' Again, 'when the rash mood –' follows the more metrical Q1; F1 has 'when the rash moode is on.'

82 (2.4.183–4) *Who . . . on't?*:   In Q1, the equivalent speech is given to Goneril ('Gonorill') who enters and says: 'Who struck my seruant, *Regan* I haue good hope / Thou didst not know ant.'

83 (2.4.194–5) *but his . . . advancement*:   'but his own faults deserved much less promotion'. 'Advancement' here means (a) 'promotion' and (b) 'thrusting forward' (like his legs in the stocks). (Cornwall's sarcasm means that the faults deserved worse punishment.)

84 (3.1.7–15) *cease . . . take all*:   This passage is in Q1. F1 has 'cease.' and lacks the remainder.

85 (3.1.22–9) *Who have . . . furnishings –*:   This passage is absent from Q1 but present in F1.

86 (3.1.32–4) *Wise . . . banner*:   'wisely taking advantage of our neglectfulness, have secretly gained a footing in our best ports, and are on the point of displaying their colours openly'.

87 (3.1.30–42) *But true . . . to you*:   This passage is present in Q1 but absent from F1.

88 (3.2.27–34) *The codpiece . . . wake*:   'The man who fornicates before he owns a home will become impoverished and lice-ridden; thus beggars "marry" both women and lice. The man who (like Lear) values what is low rather than what is truly endearing will suffer accordingly and endure sleepless nights.' The 'codpiece' (pouch for genitals) is again a metonym for 'penis'.

89 (3.2.74–7) *He . . . day*:   This verse is a variant of Feste's song ('When that I was and a little tiny boy') at the end of *Twelfth Night*. The gist is: 'Even a stupid man knows that he must submit to his circumstances.'

90 (3.2.79–96) *This . . . time*:   These lines are absent from Q1 but present in F1. (The Fool is more important as a general commentator in F1 than Q1.) The Fool's prophecy means: 'When priests offer words but not substance, when brewers adulterate their beer, when the nobility provide guidance only to their tailors, and when heretics are not burnt for heresy (though wenches' suitors burn with syphilis), then Britain will come to ruin (as at present). But when every law-case is just, no aspirant to knighthood is in debt, and there are no impoverished knights; when no slanders are uttered, no cutpurses (petty thieves) infiltrate crowds, usurers invest in crops (and thus metaphorically count their gold in the field), and pimps and whores pay for the construction of churches: then comes the time when those who live to see it will see that people will use their feet for walking –

everything will be as it should be.' Although the present lines 85–6 are, in the Folio text, located immediately after the line about bawds and whores building churches, the rearrangement improves the sense. The first six lines resemble a prophecy in William Thynne's 1532 edition of Chaucer and in George Puttenham's *Arte of English Poesie*, 1589. 'Albion' was an ancient name for Britain. According to Holinshed's *Chronicles*, Lear lived in the 8th Century BC but Merlin (the legendary prophet and wizard of King Arthur's age) lived in the 6th Century of the Christian era. Geoffrey of Monmouth's *History of the Kings of Britain* includes a lengthy collection of obscure and bizarre prophecies attributed to Merlin.

91 (3.4.17–19) *In . . . this?*: Q1 has: 'in such a night as this!'; F1 has: 'in such a night, / To shut me out? Poure on, I will endure: / In such a night as this?'.

92 (3.4.26–7) *In . . . sleep*: These lines are absent from Q1 but present in F1. Later, line 37, too, is found only in F1.

93 (3.4.36) *show . . . just*: 'make the heavens appear more just'.

94 (3.4.72) *pelican daughters*: the young pelican was believed to feed on its parent's blood.

95 (3.4.75–7) *Obey . . . array*: He refers to several of the biblical Ten Commandments (Exodus 20:3–17).

96 (3.4.93–5) *says . . . by*: mainly nonsense suitable for a Bedlamite. 'Dolphin' here is the name of a horse; *cessez* ('*Sesey*' in F1) is French for 'cease'.

97 (3.4.109) *Flibbertigibbet*: one of many devils named by Harsnett.

98 (3.4.114–18) *S'Withold . . . thee!*: 'Saint Withold walked across the wold (upland plain) three times, and met the night-goblin and her nine familiars. He enjoined her to get off (her victims) and promise (to do no more harm); and begone, witch, begone!' Q1 has 'nine fold', F1 'nine-fold'; either way, scholars are puzzled: some render it as 'nine foal', i.e. 'nine foals of a mare'. ('Mare' in the sense of 'female goblin, monster or witch' sometimes became obscured by the other sense, 'female horse'.)

99 (3.4.132–3) *But . . . year*: These lines adapt a couplet found in a 1503 version of the mediæval romance, *Sir Bevis of Hampton*.

100 (3.4.134–7) *Smulkin . . . Prince of Darkness . . . Modo . . . Mahu*: These derive from Harsnett's account of devils, though Harsnett (p. 168) terms Satan, not Modo or Mahu, 'the graund Prince of darknes'.

101 (3.4.150) *Theban*:   (a) riddle-solver, like Oedipus of Thebes; (b) wise man.

102 (3.4.173) *Athenian*:   philosopher (like Plato and Aristotle of Athens).

103 (3.4.175–7) *Childe . . . man*:   Line 175 is probably a fragment from a lost ballad about Roland, Charlemagne's nephew, hero of the *Chanson de Roland*. 'Childe' means variously 'candidate for knighthood' and 'Prince'. Lines 176–7 quote the words of the giant in the old tale of Jack the Giant-Killer, but with 'British' substituted for 'English'.

104 (3.5.5–6) *but . . . himself*:   'but a goading sense of his own merit, set to work by a reprehensible badness in Gloucester'.

105 (3.5.9) *an intelligent . . . France*:   'a spying accomplice of French interests'.

106 (3.6.6–7) *Frateretto . . . darkness*:   Frateretto is another of the devils named by Harsnett. Chaucer's 'Monk's Tale' says that the Roman emperor Nero was an angler. The 'lake of darkness' is an underworld lake: Virgil refers to 'the deep pools of Cocytus and the marsh of Styx'.

107 (3.6.12–14) *No . . . him*:   These lines are absent from Q1 but present in F1.

108 (3.6.25) *Come . . . me*:   In this line from a song, Q1 has 'broome', but editors commonly emend the word as 'burn' or 'bourn', thus making the dialogue slightly less crazy.

109 (3.6.30–32) *Hoppedance . . . thee*:   Harsnett's account of devils includes 'Hoberdidance' and cites a claim that 'croaking' in the belly may be a sign not of hunger but of a devil there (pp. 49, 195).

110 (3.6.45) *Purr . . . grey*:   'Purre' is the name of a fat devil, according to Harsnett, p. 50.

111 (3.6.17–55) *The foul . . . scape?*:   These lines are present in Q1 but absent from F1.

112 (3.6.67) *brach or him*:   'bitch or male dog'. Q1 has 'brach or him', F1 'Brache, or Hym'. Some editors emend the last word as 'lym', short for 'lyam-hound'.

113 (3.6.78) *Persian*:   'fine Persian garments' (which were often silken).

114 (3.6.83) *I'll . . . noon*:   proverbial for 'I'll play the fool, too'. This line is in F1, not Q1.

115 (3.6.99) *Thou . . . behind*:   After this line, the Fool inexplicably vanishes from the play.

116 (3.6.110–11) *When . . . thee*:   'when people who are misled, whose thoughts malign you, find that you are proven innocent and recall you for reconciliation'.

117 (3.6.95–113) *Oppressed . . . lurk*:   Kent's and Edgar's speeches are present in Q1 but absent from F1.

118 (3.7.56) *In his . . . fangs*:   Q1 has 'rash' (i.e. 'slash') where F1 has 'sticke'. A British monarch's head is traditionally anointed with holy oil at the coronation ceremony.

119 (3.7.60) *he holp . . . rain*:   'by his tears, he encouraged the skies to weep rain'. 'Holp' means 'helped'. Q1 has 'rage' where F1 has 'raine'.

120 (3.7.62–3) *Thou . . . subscribe*:   'You would have said, "Good porter, unlock the door (to let him in)"; all other cruel beings yield thus to pity'. An alternative reading of 'All cruels else subscribe' is 'whatever other forms of cruelty you endorse'.

121 (3.7.97–105) *I'll never . . . help him!*:   These lines are present in Q1 but absent from F1.

122 (4.1.6–9) *Welcome . . . blasts*:   These words are absent from Q1 but present in F1. The last two lines may mean: 'at least you never expect payment from the wretched person whom you have reduced to the worst condition'.

123 (4.1.10) *poorly led*:   Q1 originally had 'poorlie,leed'; corrected printings of Q1 have 'parti,eyd'; F1 has 'poorely led'. Some editors prefer 'parti-eyed', meaning 'with eyes of diverse colours, being gory'; others prefer 'poorly led', meaning (a) 'led by a poor man' and (b) 'led in a way unworthy of a nobleman'.

124 (4.1.12) *Life . . . age*:   'we would not be reconciled to old age (the herald of death)'.

125 (4.1.20–21) *Our means . . . commodities*:   'our assets make us complacent, while our utter defects prove to be advantageous to us'.

126 (4.1.57–62) *Five . . . master!*:   These lines are present in Q1 but absent from F1. The names of the devils in this passage again derive from Harsnett, who reports a claim that Modo haunted Sara Williams, a chambermaid, while Modu affected 'idle holy women'. 'Prince of Darkness' and 'Flibbertigibbet, of mopping and mowing' are editorial emendations of Q1's 'Prince of dumbnes' and '*Stiberdigebit* of Mobing, & *Mohing*'.

127 (4.1.66–7) *Let . . . ordinance*: 'Let the spoilt and hedonistic man who subordinates religious laws to his will'.

128 (4.2.13–15) *he'll . . . effects*: 'he'll ignore insults which call for retaliation. Our wishes may eventually become fulfilled.'

129 (4.2.17–18) *I must . . . hands*: 'At home I must exchange the insignia of the two sexes, and give the distaff (the female's symbol) to my husband (while I take up the sword, the male's symbol)'.

130 (4.2.28) *A fool . . . bed*: Earlier and later printings of this part of Q1 give (respectively) 'My foote vsurps my body' and 'A foole vsurps my bed'. F1 gives 'My Foole vsurpes my body'.

131 (4.2.38–9) *Wisdom . . . themselves*: cf. Titus 1:15: 'Vnto the pure *are* all things pure, but vnto them that are defiled, and vnbeleuing, *is* nothing pure, but euen their mindes and consciences are defiled.'

132 (4.2.31–50) *I fear . . . deep*: This important passage is present in Q1 but absent from F1.

133 (4.2.53–9) *suffering . . . so?*: This passage is present in Q1. F1 gives 'suffering.' and omits the remainder. The words 'thy state begins to threat' are an emendation of a phrase which Q1u and Q1c give (respectively) as 'thy slayer begin threats' and 'thy state begins thereat'.

134 (4.2.62) *changèd and self-covered thing*: 'thing transformed for the worse, the original self being now covered'.

135 (4.2.68) *Marry . . . mew!*: Probably: 'By St Mary, your manhood is pathetic! I mew at it (for you are as timid as a mouse scared by a cat)'.

136 (4.2.62–9) *Thou . . . news?*: These lines of dialogue are present in Q1 but absent from F1.

137 (4.2.85–7) *May . . . tart*: 'may pull all my castles in the air down upon my detestable life (with Albany). From another point of view, the news is not so bitter' (perhaps because Edmund, whom she may yet win, will gain much of Cornwall's power).

138 (4.3) *SCENE 3*: This scene is present in Q1 but absent from F1.

139 (4.3.29) *Let . . . it!*: This is an emendation of Q1's 'Let pitie not be beleeft'.

140 (4.3.31) *That clamour moistened*: 'in which her outcry had induced tears'. This is an emendation of Q1's 'And clamour moystened her'. (RF prefers 'And clamour mastered her'.)

141 (4.4.10) *take . . . worth*: 'take as reward all my material possessions'.

142 (4.4.23–4) *O . . . about*: In Luke 2:49, Jesus says: '[K]newe ye not that I must go about my fathers busines?'

143 (4.5.20–21) *Belike . . . what*: Regan is in a state of uncertainty. She may be speculating about the contents of the letter or about ways of persuading Oswald.

144 (4.5.33) *give him this*: The item may be a favour (a love-token) or a letter.

145 (4.6.23–4) *Lest . . . headlong*: 'lest I become dizzy and my failing sight cause me to fall headlong'.

146 (4.6.37–40) *and not . . . out*: 'and not descend to quarrelling with your irresistible will, the smouldering candle-stub of my life (its detested remainder) would burn itself out': i.e., 'I would live on, however wretchedly, if it were possible to do so without impiously impugning the gods'. 'Snuff ' normally meant the blackened part of the candle-wick.

147 (4.6.71) *Horns . . . sea*: 'horns twisted in spirals like a whelk-shell and wavy like the angry sea'. Q1 has 'enridged', F1 'enraged'.

148 (4.6.73–4) *the clearest . . . impossibilities*: 'the immaculate gods, who gain honour by doing what would be impossible for men'.

149 (4.6.81–2) *the safer . . . thus*: 'a sane mind would never make its owner dress like this'.

150 (4.6.91) *i'th'clout: hewgh!*: 'in the centre of the target: whoosh!' (He imitates the sound of an arrow in flight.)

151 (4.6.98–100) *To say . . . divinity*: 'To agree with everything I said (whether it was right or wrong) was not good theology.' (There is an echo of 2 Corinthians 1.17–20, particularly verse 19: 'For the Sonne of God . . . was not Yea, and Nay: but in him it was Yea.')

152 (4.6.119–20) *whose . . . virtue*: 'whose face suggests that between her legs she is pure as snow, who affectedly seems virtuous'.

153 (4.6.122–32) *the fitchew . . . thee*: Q1 prints the whole of Lear's speech as prose; F1 changes it from verse to prose at 'Behold' (line 118). The rhythmic insistence of lines 122–32 solicits their treatment as flexible verse. The speech's misogyny may have been aided by Harsnett, who, on pp. 50 and 141, reports the

allegations that Sara Williams, possessed by devils, 'had all hell in her belly' and that her 'namelesse part' was 'the deuils port-gate'.

154 (4.6.165–70) *Plate . . . lips*:   This passage is absent from Q1 but present in F1.

155 (4.6.170–72) *Get . . . not*:   Although editors usually claim that 'glass eyes' are spectacles, the reference is obviously to prosthetic glass eyes (which would lend the appearance of sight to someone who does not see) rather than to spectacles (which would improve the sight of a person with impaired vision). Ambrose Paré (1510–90) developed artificial eyes of gold and silver, and M. O. Hughes' 'History of Artificial Eyes' (website) quotes these lines of *King Lear* as confirmation that glass eyes were in use by the time of the play's writing.

156 (4.6.197–8) *Ay . . . bridegroom*:   Line 197 is present in Q1 but absent from F1. Line 198 means: 'like a spruce bridegroom, I shall (a) die heroically; (b) die splendidly dressed; (c) have a splendid orgasm'.

157 (4.6.206–7) *the general . . . to*:   The 'twain' may be: (a) Adam and Eve, who brought original sin to the world; or, less likely, (b) Goneril and Regan.

158 (4.6.213–14) *the main . . . thought*:   'we expect to see the main body any hour now'.

159 (4.6.225–6) *The bounty . . . boot!*:   'May the generosity and blessings of Heaven reward you, in addition to my thanks!'

160 (4.6.235) *Chill . . . cagion*:   (in Somerset dialect:) 'I won't let go, sir, without better cause.'

161 (4.6.237–41) *Good . . . harder*:   'Good gentleman, go on your way, and let poor people proceed. If I could have been killed by bullying bluster, my life would have been a fortnight shorter than it is. No, don't approach the old man; keep away, I warn you, or I shall find out whether your head or my cudgel is the harder.' In line 241, 'ballow' (a dialectal word) corresponds to F1's 'Ballow'. Q1u has 'battero', and Q1c has 'bat', so some editors read 'baton'.

162 (4.6.244–5) *no matter . . . foins*:   'your thrusts don't matter'.

163 (4.6.260–61) *we rip . . . lawful*:   'we torture them until their hearts are torn; tearing open their papers is less immoral'.

164 (4.6.269) *and for . . . venture*:   These obscure words are present in Q1 but absent from F1. They may mean: (a) 'and as far as you

are concerned, she is her own woman (not Albany's wife) to venture for you'; or (b) 'and, whatever the risk, she chooses to dedicate herself to you'.

165 (4.6.271) *O . . . will!*: 'Oh, indefinable extent of a woman's desires!'

166 (4.7) SCENE 7: In Q1, the speaking characters in this scene are five: Cordelia, Kent, the doctor, a gentleman and Lear. In F1, there are four, as the doctor's rôle is allocated to a gentleman (who retains the physician's expertise); and Kent's concluding dialogue with the gentleman is cut. In lines 90–91, the latter's reference to Kent's being in Germany may seem inconsistent with line 1, in which Cordelia addresses Kent by name; but the opening dialogue can easily be enacted as a private one which is not overheard by the gentleman. In the edition by René Weis (1993), the doctor and the gentleman do not enter until after line 11.

167 (4.7.24–5) *Very . . . there*: These words are present in Q1 but absent from F1.

168 (4.7.33–6) *To stand . . . helm?*: These lines are present in Q1 but absent from F1. The phrase 'poor perdu' (from French *perdu*, 'lost',) means a lost or abandoned person; and *sentinelle perdue* is French for a sentinel or watchman in a perilously-exposed location. The 'thin helm' (light helmet) is Lear's hair.

169 (4.7.39–40) *hovel thee . . . straw*: The phrasing recalls the biblical story of the Prodigal Son (Luke 15:11–32).

170 (4.7.46–7) *I am . . . fire*: In Greek legend, Ixion in the underworld was bound to a wheel of fire by Zeus; in Christian tradition, to suffer on a burning wheel is one of the punishments of the damned.

171 (4.7.79–82) *it is . . . settling*: 'it is dangerous to make him fill the gaps in his memory. Ask him to go in; don't disturb him further until he is more composed.' Lines 79–80, from 'and yet' to 'lost', are present in Q1 but absent from F1.

172 (4.7.86–96) *Holds . . . fought*: These lines are present in Q1 but absent from F1. The concluding couplet means: 'The culmination and end of my career will be completely shaped, for better or for worse, by today's battle.'

173 (5.1.8) *Tell . . . truth*: 'Tell me only the truth – but then tell me all the truth'.

174 (5.1.11–13) *That . . . hers*: These words are present in Q1 but absent from F1. Regan's speech means: 'I fear that you have been joined and intimate with her to the fullest extent.'

175 (5.1.18–19) *I . . . me*: These words are present in Q1 but absent from F1.

176 (5.1.23–8) *Where . . . nobly*: This passage is present in Q1 but absent from F1. Lines 25–7 mean: 'It concerns us insofar as the King of France invades our land, and not because he emboldens King Lear and others who, I fear, have fair and strong grounds for opposing us.'

177 (5.1.37) *I . . . riddle*: The 'riddle' is: 'Why should a hostile sister, Regan, seek Goneril's company?' The answer is: 'So that Goneril can't seek Edmund's'.

178 (5.2. S.D.) *Alarum . . . Exeunt*: In Q1, the S.D. here is: '*Alarum. Enter the powers of France ouer the stage, Cordelia with her father in her hand.*' In F1, the equivalent S.D. is: '*Alarum within. Enter with Drumme and Colours, Lear, Cordelia, and Souldiers, ouer the Stage, and Exeunt.*'

179 (5.2.9–11) *Men . . . all*: 'People must submit to death as to birth: in both cases, what matters is to be ripe for the occasion.' (Thus premature death, suicide, is as inappropriate as premature birth.)

180 (5.3.17–19) *we'll . . . moon*: 'we'll outlive cliques and factions of great people who, like the moon-governed tides, flow in and out (of fame, favour or prosperity)'.

181 (5.3.22–3) *He . . . foxes*: 'The man who separates us will have to take a firebrand from heaven and drive us apart like foxes (when they are smoked out of their holes or when their tails are on fire).' The phrasing distantly recalls (a) Prometheus, who stole fire from heaven, (b) Harsnett's reference to men who 'smoke out a Foxe out of his burrow' (p. 89), and (c) Samson, who (according to Judges 15:3–8) attached firebrands to foxes' tails in order to ignite the cornfields of the Philistines.

182 (5.3.39–40) *I . . . do't*: This speech is present in Q1 but absent from F1.

183 (5.3.55–60) *At . . . place*: This passage is present in Q1 but absent from F1.

184 (5.3.71) *That . . . you*: This line is allocated to Goneril by Q1 but to Albany by F1.

185 (5.3.77) *Dispose . . . thine*: This line is absent from Q1 but present in F1. I substitute 'are' for F1's 'is'.

186 (5.3.80) *The let-alone . . . will*: 'The power of preventing it, Goneril, is not a matter of your wish or desire.'

187 (5.3.82) *Let . . . thine*: 'Let the drum beat as signal for a duel, so that you can prove (by fighting Albany) that you and I are united.' In Q1 the line is given to Edmund (addressing Albany) and reads: 'Let the drum strike, and proue my title good.'

188 (5.3.143) *What . . . delay*: This line is absent from Q1 but present in F1.

189 (5.3.147–9) *Which . . . ever*: 'and because, as yet, these tossed-back accusations of treason glance off and scarcely cause a bruise, my sword will give them immediate and direct passage to the place (your heart) where they will remain for ever'.

190 (5.3.157) *the laws are mine*: Because she is the senior heiress of a king, she claims to control the laws like a queen. (At 1.1.126–38, however, Lear had handed over power specifically to Albany and Cornwall.)

191 (5.3.158) Exit.: In F1, her exit is here. In Q1, her exit is a line or so later, after her words 'Aske me not what I know.' As she has previously recognised the letter, F1, which ascribes those words to Edmund, makes more sense.

192 (5.3.203–6) *This . . . extremity*: 'To people who dislike sorrow, this would have seemed a time to conclude; and only one more sorrow, amplifying the theme too much, would be excessive and surpass the limit.' (Yet Edgar will proceed to that excess.)

193 (5.3.203–20) *This . . . slave*: This passage is present in Q1 but absent from F1.

194 (5.3.250) *Haste . . . life!*: In Q1 this speech is given to Albany and is addressed to Edgar, who apparently (there being no S.D. here in Q1) then hastens away with the sword and returns with Lear and Cordelia. In F1 the speech is given to Edgar, who apparently gives the sword to a gentleman to take to the offstage captain. Some editors assume that the captain is already present on stage and receives the sword directly from Edgar.

195 (5.3.262) *the promised end?*: i.e. the Doomsday foretold in the Gospels and the Book of Revelation.

196 (5.3.263) *Fall and cease!*: 'Let the heavens fall and all things end!'

197 (5.3.264) *This . . . so*: I preserve the punctuation of F1. Q1 has: 'This feather stirs she liues, if it be so,'. Either way, the opening seems conditional, meaning: '*If* the feather moves, she's alive . . . '

Some editors, however, emend the punctuation to suggest that, for a moment, Lear believes that Cordelia is indeed alive: for example, the Norton conflated text (1997) gives: 'This feather stirs; she lives!'

198 (5.3.281) *This . . . sight*: These words are absent from Q1 but present in F1.

199 (5.3.304) *And my . . . hanged!*: Editors customarily explain that 'fool' could be a term of endearment and that the reference is therefore to Cordelia, not the Fool; and this reading is supported by the context. Nevertheless, the term brings the Fool to mind, and renders conspicuous his absence from Acts 4 and 5.

200 (5.3.309–10) *Do you . . . dies.*: These words are absent from Q1 but present in F1. They suggest that Lear, when at the brink of death, thinks he sees a sign that Cordelia is still alive. In Q1, immediately after 'thanke you sir,' Lear says 'O, o, o, o.'; and the sentence 'Breake hart, I prethe breake.' is allocated to Lear, not Kent.

201 (5.3.319) *Rule . . . sustain*: This may mean that Kent and Edgar are being asked (a) to rule the realm jointly with Albany; (b) to rule the realm, Albany not wishing to rule; or (c) to wield power as noblemen, thus helping Albany to regenerate the deeply-wounded ('gored') state.

202 (5.3.322–5) *The weight . . . long*: Q1 allots this speech to Albany, F1 to Edgar. Since Albany has offered power to Kent and Edgar, and Kent has responded, it is now, logically, Edgar's turn to respond. The words mean: 'We must shoulder the burden at this sad time; and we must say what we feel, not what we should conventionally say on such an occasion. And what we feel is that the older generation [or the oldest person, Lear,] has borne most; we who are young shall never see such sights, nor shall we live so long.' (Presumably the young will be short-lived because they have been sapped by their recent experiences.)

GLOSSARY

Where a pun or an ambiguity occurs, the meanings are distinguished as (a) and (b), or (a), (b) and (c), etc. Otherwise, alternative meanings are distinguished as (i) and (ii), or as (i), (ii) and (iii), etc. Abbreviations include the following: adj., adjective; adv., adverb; cf., compare; conj., conjunction; dial., dialectal; e.g., for example; fig., figurative; Fr., French; lit., literally; *O.E.D.*, *Oxford English Dictionary*; p.p.: past participle; S.D., stage direction; vb., verb.

abhorred: abhorrent.

able (vb.): empower.

abominable: inhuman.

abroad: (i: 1.2.163:) out of doors; (ii: 2.1.6:) currently spreading.

abuse: (i: 2.4.302; 4.1.22; 4.7.53, 77:) deceive, delude; (ii: 3.7.89:) treat unjustly; (iii: 4.7.15:) ill-treat; (iv: 5.1.11:) dishonour.

accent: mode of speech.

accommodate: clothe, equip

act: 2.1.18: do.

action-taking: litigious.

addition: titles of honour.

advise: persuade; **advise oneself**: consider.

affect: (i: 1.1.1:) favour, prefer; (ii: 2.1.97: a) influence; (b) incline; (iii: 2.2.91: a) display; (b) feign.

ague: 4.6.105: (a) fever; (b) shivering fit.

aidant: helpful.

alarum: (i: 5.2. S.D.:) noise of battle; (ii: 5.3. S.D.:) noise of battlefield instruments (e.g. trumpet-calls).

alarumed: roused to action.

Albany: (i:) land north of the river Humber; (ii:) Duke of Albany.

Albion: Britain.

all (adv.): (i: 1.1.103:) exclusively; (ii: 4.7.42:) completely; (iii: 5.3.53:) exactly.

allay: abate, subside.

allow: (i: 2.4.186:) approve of; (ii: 3.7.103): lend.

alone: 1.1.74: only.

alteration: changes of mind.

amazed: bewildered.

an (conj.): if.

anatomize: dissect.

ancient: (i: 1.2.140; 4.1.43:) long-established; (ii: 2.2.57; 2.2.121:) elderly; **ancient of**

war: officers experienced in warfare.

answer (vb.): (i: 2.2.141:) be responsible for; (ii: 3.4.96:) encounter.

Apollo: the classical sun-god.

apprehend: 2.1.107: arrest, capture.

approve: prove, confirm.

arbitrement: decisive contest.

arch (noun): chief, master.

argument: subject, theme.

aroint thee!: be gone!

arraign: call to account.

array (noun): clothing.

art: (i: 3.2.70:) transformative power; (ii: 4.6.222:) experience.

asquint: distortedly.

attaint: **in thine attaint**: as accomplice of your treason.

attasked: taken to task, rebuked.

attempt: 2.2.117: assault.

attend: (i: 1.1.33:) wait upon; (ii: 2.1.124; 2.4.35; 5.1.33:) await; (iii: 2.3.5:) seek.

auricular: audible.

avaunt: away.

avouch: declare to be true.

away: 2.2.133: hither, here.

a-work: to work.

aye: 5.3.234: for ever.

back: 4.2.90: on the way back.

ballow: cudgel.

ban: curse.

bandy looks: glare back.

barber-monger: fop.

base: 1.2.6: (a) illegitimate; (b) low, inferior.

battle: 3.2.23: army.

bawd: pimp.

beadle: parish officer who whipped malefactors.

bear (vb.): (i: 1.1.301:) sustain, exhibit; (ii: 4.2.51; 4.6.80:) maintain.

bearing: 3.6.105: endurance.

beat: 3.4.14: throb.

become: 4.3.24: grace, adorn.

bedlam (noun): 3.7.101: vagabond who is mad or purports to be mad. (**Tom o'Bedlam**: name assumed by such a vagabond.)

Bedlam (adj.): supposedly from the hospital of St Mary of Bethlehem, an asylum.

beguile: (i: 2.2.105:) deceive; (ii: 4.6.63; 5.3.153:) cheat, outwit.

be it: 1.1.252: if it be.

belike: probably.

belly-pinchèd: starving.

bemadding: maddening.

bench (vb.): sit on a bench in a law-court.

bend: 2.1.45; 4.2.74: direct.

benefit (noun): pleasure.

benison: blessing.

bereavèd: 4.4.9: lost.

besort: befit.

bestow: 2.4.283; 4.6.283: accommodate.

bethought: 2.3.6: resolved.

bewray: reveal.

bias of nature: natural inclination.

bide: endure.

biding: abode.

big: 5.3.207: loud.

bill: **brown bill**: halberd, painted brown to prevent rust.

bitter: (i: 1.4.126:) biting, sarcastic; (ii: 1.4.128, 134: a) embittered; (b) pitiable.

blank: white spot at the centre of an archery-target; **blank of thine eye**: object to be noted.

blast (noun): (i: 1.4.286:) infectious or withering air; (ii: 3.6.43:) cry; (iii: 4.1.9:) stormy gust.

blast (vb.): 2.4.163: strike down.

block: 4.6.183: (probably) hatter's mould; hence, head.

blood: (i: 3.1.40:) noble descent; (ii: 3.4.160; 3.5.21; 5.3.166:) lineage, kinship; (iii: 4.2.64:) passion, anger.

blown: 4.4.27: inflated with pride.

bobtail: with tail cut short.

bold (vb.): embolden.

bond: 1.1.92; 2.4.173: tie of duty to a parent.

boon: requested favour.

boot: 5.3.300: added reward; **to boot, and boot**: (perhaps) in addition and as a reward.

bootless: fruitless.

bo-peep: game like 'Hide and Seek'.

border (vb.): confine, keep.

bordered in itself: kept within bounds.

bosom: **of her bosom**: in her confidence; **the common bosom**: popularity.

bosomed: breast to breast, intimate.

bound: (i: 3.7.7:) obliged; (ii: 3.7.10:) committed.

bourn: (i: 3.6.25:) river; (ii: 4.6.57:) boundary-cliff.

brach: bitch-hound (*O.E.D.*).

brave: 3.2.79: splendid; **bravely**: 4.6.198: (a) courageously; (b) in fine attire.

brazed: brazened, hardened.

breath: 1.4.120: utterance.

bred: 4.2.73: brought up (from childhood).

breeding: upbringing.

broken meats: left-overs, scraps of food.

buoy up: surge up.

burn (vb.): 3.2.84: (a) execute by fire; (b) pain by venereal disease.

butterflies: **gilded butterflies**: dandified courtiers.

buzz (noun): rumour.

cadent: falling.

cage: 5.3.9: (a) bird-cage; (b) prison.

caitiff: wretch.

canker-bit: worm-eaten.

capable of: 2.1.84: qualified to inherit.

carbonado: slash.

carbuncle: tumour.

carry: (i: 1.1.300:) wield; (ii: 3.2.48:) endure; (iii: 5.3.37:) contrive; **carry out my side**: keep my promise.

case: **case of eyes**: eye-sockets; **heavy case**: sad plight.

casement: hinged window.

casualty: uncertainty.

cataracts: deluges.

catastrophe: dénouement, outcome.

cause: (i: 4.3.51:) affair; (ii: 4.6.109) alleged offence in law.

censure (vb.): judge critically.

centaur: mythical creature, half human and half horse.

century: unit of 100 foot-soldiers.

certain (adj.): safe, reliable.

certain (adv.): with certainty.

cessez (Fr.): stop.

challenge: 1.1.52; 4.7.31: claim as due.

champains: open plains.

character: 1.2.60; 2.1.71: handwriting.

charge (noun): (i: 1.2.123:) responsibility; (ii: 2.4.234:) expense.

charge (vb.): (i: 2.1.50:) thrust a weapon at; (ii: 4.5.18:) stress.

chatter: **make me chatter**: make my teeth chatter.

che (dial.): I.

Childe: title of a noble youth.

child-like: befitting a dutiful son.

chill (dial.): I will.

choleric: irascible.

chough: kind of crow, e.g. jackdaw.

chud (dial.): I would.

civet: perfume derived from civet-cat.

clamour: cries of grief.

clap: **at a clap**: at a stroke.

clearest: 4.6.73: purest.

closet: private room.

clothier's yard: 37 inches; about the length of an arrow.

clotpoll: blockhead.

clout (noun): target in archery.

cock: (i: 3.2.3:) weather-cock; (4.6.19:) small boat.

cockney: over-refined woman.

codpiece: (i: 3.2.40:) pouch, at the front of hose or breeches, to hold penis and scrotum; hence (ii: 3.2.27:) penis.

cohort: company of soldiers.

coining: minting coins.

cold: **catch cold**: become cold (not 'catch a cold').

colour: 2.2.132: character.

Come your ways!: Come on!

comfort (noun): assistance.

comfort (vb.): help.

comfortable: comforting.

commend: (i: 2.4.27:) deliver; (ii: 3.1.19:) entrust.

commit: 3.4.76: commit adultery.

commodities: advantages.

compáct (vb.): confirm.

compáct (p.p.): knit together.

compáct (adj.): in league.

compeer (vb.): equal.

compliment: polite ceremony.

composition: 2.2.19: combination; **more composition**: 1.2.12: better constitution.

compounded: copulated.

conceit: imagination.

conceive: (i: 1.1.11-12: a) understand; (b) become pregnant by; (ii: 4.2.24:) imagine.

condition: character, disposition.

conduct (noun): guidance.

conduct (vb.): lead, command.

conductor: leader, commander.

confederacy: conspiracy.

confine (noun): 2.4.143: allotted span.

confine (vb.): limit.

confusion: ruin.

conjunct: closely joined.

consort: company.

constant: fixed; **constant pleasure**: settled preference.

constrain: strain, force.

contemned: despised.

continent (noun): container.

continent (adj.): controlled.

convenience: favourable circumstances.

convenient: (i: 3.2.56: a) proper; (b) appropriate; (ii: 4.5.31; 5.1.36:) fitting.

converse with: associate with.

convey: manage discreetly.

cope: encounter.

corky: 3.7.28: (a) weak and withered; (b) dried up.

costard: large apple; hence (fig.), head.

couch (vb.): lie low.

counsel: **keep honest counsel**: keep honourable secrets.

countenance: (i: 1.2.151; 1.4.25:) appearance; (ii: 5.1.63:) authority.

course (noun): (i: 3.7.52) series of attacks; (ii: 3.7.99:) regular process; (iii: 4.2.94:) range.

course . . . for (vb.): 3.4.55: hunt . . . as.

court holy-water: (fig.) flattery.

court'sy: **do a court'sy**: 3.7.25: make a bow; hence, yield.

cowish: timid.

coxcomb: (i: 1.4.88, etc.:) jester's cap, crested like a cock's comb; (ii, fig.: 2.4.118–19:) head.

cozen (vb.) : cheat.

cozener: person who cheats.

crab: crab-apple (sour and wild).

credit: trustworthiness.

croak: 3.6.31: rumble.

cross (noun): adversity.

cross-lightning: zigzag or forked lightning.

crow-keeper: boy with bow and arrows, to protect crops from crows.

cruels: 3.7.63: (a) cruel beings; (b) forms of cruelty.

cry: 3.2.58: beg for; **cry out**: 5.1.23: protest.

cub-drawn: sucked dry; hence, ravenous.

cuckoo-flower: perhaps Lady's Smock or Ragged Robin.

cullionly: scoundrelly.

Cupid: **blind Cupid**: blind-folded god of love.

curiosity: (i: 1.1.5:) scrupulous inspection; (ii: 1.2.4:) fastidiousness; (iii: 1.4.64:) suspicious concern.

curious: 1.4.30: (a) elaborate; (b) subtle.

curst: angry.

cut: 4.6.193: slit, cut open.

cutpurse: thief who cuts purses from belts, etc.

darker: 1.1.35: more secret.

darkling: in the dark.

darnel: 4.4.5: (a) grassy weed that grows in cornfields; (b) poppy.

daub it: pretend.

deadly: (i: 4.2.36:) entailing death; (ii: 5.3.289:) death-like.

dead march: stately music suitable for a funeral.

dear: (i: 1.1.181; 1.4.259:) precious; (ii: 2.4.96:) a) affectionate; (b) beloved; (iii: 3.1.19; 4.3.44, 51:) important; (iv: 4.4.28:) deep.

dearn: dire.

death-practised: whose death has been plotted.

deathsman: executioner.

deed: 1.1.70: (a) true contract; (b) enactment.

deer: 3.4.132: animals.

dejected: humbled.

delicate: (i: 3.4.12; 4.3.13:) sensitive; (ii: 4.6.184:) ingenious.

demand (noun): enquiry.

demand (vb.): enquire, ask.

deny: refuse.

depend: 1.4.236: be dependent (on Lear).

depositary: trustee.

derogate: degenerate.

descent: 5.3.136: lowest part.

descry (noun): sighting.

desperate: 2.4.300: reckless.

desperately: 5.3.291: in despair.

detested: detestable.

dialect: manner of speech peculiar to a person or theme (not necessarily local).

difference: 1.4.82–3: distinction of rank.

diffidence: suspicion.

diffuse: disguise.

digest: amalgamate.

dimensions: bodily parts.

disaster: 1.1.173: misfortune.

disclaim in: deny all share in.

discover: 2.1.65: expose, unmask.

discovery: 5.1.53: reconnaissance.

dismantle: strip off.

disnatured: lacking in natural affection.

disposition: tendency or inclination.

dissipation: breaking up.

distaff: stick holding material to be spun.

distaste (vb.): dislike.

distract (adj.): mad.

distribution: 4.1.69: (a) sharing out; (perhaps b) administration of justice.

divine thrusting on: compulsion by the gods.

division: 1.2.132: (a) discord; (b) musical variation.

doubt: fear.

doubtful: suspicious.

dower: dowry.

Dragon: constellation Draco.

draw: 1.1.84; 3.3.21: win.

dwell in: 2.4.181: depend on.

each: at each: (probably) end to end.

ear-kissing: whispered.

earnest of: initial payment for.

earnestly: zealously.

effect: to effect: in importance.

effects: (i: 1.1.130; 2.4.174:) outward manifestations; (ii: 4.2.15:) accomplished facts; (iii: 1.1.184; 1.2.138:) results.

element: 2.4.56: appropriate
place. -

elf (vb.): tangle.

eliads (from Fr. *œillades*):
amorous glances.

embossèd: swollen.

engine: 1.4.255: (a) lever;
(b) device or mechanism.

enguard: surround as if to guard.

enormous: 2.2.163: (a) monstrous; (b) abnormal.

entertain: (i: 1.4.53:) treat;
(ii: 3.6.76:) take into service.

epicurism: gluttony.

esperance: hope.

essay: assay, trial.

estate: condition.

event: outcome.

evidence: their evidence:
evidence against them.

excellent: 1.2.114: extreme,
utter.

execution: direction.

exeunt: they go out.

exhibition: grant of money for
maintenance.

exit: he or she goes out.

expense: squandering.

extremity: (i: 3.4.97:) extreme
violence; (ii: 5.3.206:) the
utmost limit.

fain (adj.): glad.

fain (adv.): gladly.

faint: 1.4.63: (a) lazy; (b) slight.

faithed: believed.

falchion: curved broadsword.

fall into taint: bring into
discredit.

fastened: 2.1.76: confirmed.

favour: 4.2.21, S.D.: token of
affection and support.

favours: 3.7.39: facial features:
here, beard.

fears (vb.): 3.5.3: frightens.

feature: physical appearance.

feel: 1.2.82: assess.

feeling (adj.): 4.6.222: heartfelt.

feelingly: 4.6.149: (a) by touch;
(b) intensely.

felicitate: made happy.

fell: flesh and fell: meat and
skin: entirely.

femiter: fumitory: sprawling
weed.

festinate: speedy.

fetch (noun): lying excuse.

field: open countryside.

fierce: 1.2.12: energetic, ardent.

find: (i: 1.2.48:) detect;
(ii: 2.4.191:) deem to be so.

finical: over-fastidious.

fire-new: brand-new.

fit (adv.): suitably.

fitchew: polecat.

fitly: at a suitable time; fitly
like: 1.1.199: aptly please.

fitness: my fitness: proper for
me.

fixed: 3.4.8: rooted.

flake: lock of hair.

flash (vb.): break out.

flaw (noun): fragment.

flawed (adj.): damaged,
cracked.

flesh (vb.): 2.2.42: initiate in
bloodshed.

flesh and fell: entirely.

fleshment: excitement of
initiation.

flourish: fanfare.

flying off: desertion.

foin (noun): fencer's thrust.

following: 2.2.144: attending to.

fond: foolish.

Fool: professional jester.

fool: (i) foolish person;
(ii: 3.2.41: a) foolish person;
(b) professional jester;
(iii: 5.3.304:) dear one; **moral
fool**: moralising idiot; **natural
fool**: congenital simpleton.

foot (vb.): (i: 3.3.12; 3.7.44:)
gain a foothold; (ii: 3.4.114:)
walk over.

fop: foolish man.

foppery: foolishness.

foppish: foolish.

forbear: (i: 1.2.154:) avoid;
(ii: 2.4.104:) restrain myself.

forbearance: patience.

fordo: destroy.

fore-vouched: previously-
professed.

forfended: forbidden.

fork: 1.1.143: barbed arrow-
head; **forked**: two-legged;
forks: 4.6.119: pair of legs.

forlorn: wretched.

form: 3.7.24: formal procedure.

Fortune: Fortuna, Roman deity
of chance; **at Fortune's alms**:
as a fortuitous charitable gift.

fortune: chance; **sick in fortune**: unlucky.

frame (vb.): construct.

frank: generous.

free: (i: 2.3.3.:) unguarded;
(ii: 3.4.11; 3.6.103; 4.6.80:)
carefree.

fret: 1.4.272: form by erosion.

fretful: 3.1.4: (a) turbulent;
(b) angry.

from: (i: 2.2.93:) contrary to;

(ii: 2.1.123; 2.4.200, 285:)
away from; **give from**:
1.1.124-5: withdraw from.

frontlet: band on forehead;
hence, frown.

fruitfully: plentifully.

furnishings: decorations.

furred gown: formal gown, as
worn by judges, clergy, etc.

furrow-weeds: weeds growing
on ploughed land.

Fut!: (a, Fr.) *foutre!* (fuck!);
(b) By God's (or Christ's)
foot!

gad: sharp spike, goad; **upon
the gad**: suddenly.

gale: breeze (*O.E.D.*).

gall (noun): 1.4.105: cause of
bitterness.

gallow: terrify.

garb: style of speech or manner.

gasted: frightened.

gate: way; **go your gate**: hurry
away.

general: **general curse**: sin
incurred by the human race;
general dependants: all the
dependants.

generation: offspring.

generous: nobly great.

gentle: (i: 4.6.208:) noble;
(ii: 4.6.217:) merciful.

gentleman: well-bred man-
servant.

germen: seed.

get: 1.2.15; 2.1.77; 3.4.139;
4.6.116: beget

girdle: waist.

give from: 1.1.124-5: withdraw
from.

give him way: let him go.

glass eyes: prosthetic eyes made of glass.

glass-gazing: mirror-gazing, vain.

glove: 3.4.81: woman's glove worn as pledge.

go: 1.4.112: walk; **go to** (1.4.84: a) hurry off; (b) see sense; **goes to't**: copulates.

goatish: lustful.

goodman boy: young upstart.

gosmore: gossamer: filmy web-strands.

got: 2.1.77: begot.

grace: (i: 1.1.57:) attractiveness; (ii: 1.1.228, 264, 271:) favour; (iii: 5.2.4:) divine favour; (iv: 2.2.126:) honour; (v: 3.2.40 a:) nobility; (b) wisdom; (vi: 3.2.59:) mercy; (vii: 5.3.68:) good qualities.

graced, gracious: dignified, honourable.

greet the time: be ready.

gross: (i: 1.3.5:) flagrant; (ii: 4.6.14:) large.

grossly: obviously.

guardian: steward.

halcyon: kingfisher; **halcyon beaks**: 2.2.73: compliant natures.

half-blooded: 5.3.81: (a) with only one parent of noble blood; (b) illegitimate.

handy-dandy: take your choice.

haply: 1.1.99: (a) perhaps; (b) happily.

happy: (i: 2.3.2:) opportune; (ii: 4.6.72, 226; 5.3.36:) fortunate.

hardock: 'coarse weedy plant: probably burdock' (*O.E.D.*).

hatch: lower half of a divided door.

head-lugged: dragged by the head.

headier: more headstrong.

heat: i'th'heat: quickly.

heavy: (i: 4.6.147:) grievous; (ii: 5.1.27:) important.

Heccat: Hecate, goddess of the underworld and witchcraft.

heels: **grow out at heels**: become worn-out.

hell-hated: hateful as hell.

high-engendered: created in the heavens.

high-judging: 2.4.223: (a) judging in heaven; (b) acting as supreme judge.

hit (vb.): 1.1.299: (a) agree; (b) strike.

hizzing: hissing.

Hóla, hóla!: 5.3.72: (a) Stop, stop!; (b: cry of derision:) Ho, indeed!

hold: 5.3.154: (a) stop; (b) wait; (c) take this.

holla (vb.): call.

hollowness: 1.1.153: (a) insincerity; (b) vacuity; 1.2.108: insincerity.

holp: helped.

holy-water: water blessed by a priest; **court holy-water**: flattery.

home (adv.): 3.3.11; 3.4.16: thoroughly; **charges home**: thrusts directly at.

honest: 1.2.9: chaste.

honoured: honourable.

horn: 3.6.73: drinking-horn.
horseway: bridle-path.
hospitable: belonging to a host.
hurricano: waterspout.
Ice (dial.): I shall.
idle: (i: 1.2.48; 1.3.17:) foolish;
(ii: 4.4.5; 4.6.21:) useless.
ignorance: stupidity.
image: exact picture, close
description.
immediacy: direct relationship.
impatience: loss of self-control.
impertinency: 4.6.174: (a)
irrelevance; (b) nonsense.
import (vb.): signify.
important: importunate.
impressed: conscripted.
in-a-door: indoors.
incense (vb.): incite.
incline to: side with.
indistinguished: indefinable.
infirmity: (i: 1.1.201; 289:)
defect; (ii: 2.4.101:) sickness.
inflamed: passionate.
ingenious: fully conscious.
ingraffed: engrafted, implanted.
inherit: possess.
innocent (noun): 3.6.7: simpleton, fool.
insult (vb.): 2.2.114: exult.
intelligence: 2.1.21: information.
intelligent: informative.
interessed: **be interessed**: lay claim.
interest of: legal claim to.
interlude: comedy, farce.
intrince: tightly knotted.
invention: plan.
issue: (i: 1.1.16: a) offspring; (b)
outcome; (ii: 1.4.3:) outcome.
it (as possessive adj.): its.
jakes: lavatory, privy.

jealous: 1.4.64; 5.1.56: suspi-
ciously watchful.
jewel: darling.
joint-stool: stool made by a
joiner.
Jug: 1.4.212: (a) nickname of
Joan; (b) slang for maid-
servant, sweetheart or sexual
partner; (c) jug of ale.
Jupiter: the supreme Roman
deity.
justicer: judge.
kibe: 1.5.8: chapped or ulcer-
ated chilblain (*O.E.D.*).
kind (adj.): naturally affectionate.
kindly: 1.5.12: (a) with natural
affection; (b) according to her
nature.
knap: rap.
knave: (i: 1.1.20; 1.4.40, 89;
3.2.72:) boy; (ii: 1.4.75;
1.4.86:) servant; (iii: 1.4.301;
2.2.13, 19; 2.4.81:) scoundrel.
knee (vb.): kneel before.
labours: **full of labours**: admirably diligent.
lag of: later than.
large: (i: 1.1.51:) generous;
(ii: 1.1.130:) splendid;
(iii: 1.1.183:) lavish.
latched: caught.
late (adj.): 1.2.99: recent.
late (adv.): 2.2.111: recently.
lendings: lent items.
let-alone: 5.3.80: power to
intervene.
light on: see.
like (vb.): 1.1.199: please.
likeness: 1.4.4: recognisable
appearance.
lily-livered: cowardly.

list (vb.): (i: 5.3.62:) please;
(ii: 5.3.180:) listen to.

lists: roster.

litter: portable bed.

living: 1.4.100: property, lands.

lodging: accommodation for
the night.

long-ingraffed: long-engrafted:
habitual.

look: 3.3.13: seek; look about:
take stock.

looped: with loopholes.

loose: 1.4.290: let flow.

louse (vb.): become infested
with lice.

lubber: clumsy lout.

lurk: hide.

lust-dieted: 4.1.66: (a) glutted
on sensual pleasures;
(b) pleasure-craving.

lusty: 1.2.11: (a) lustful;
(b) vigorous.

luxury: lechery.

machination: plotting.

made intent: planned purpose.

main: 3.1.6: mainland.

mainly: 4.7.65: entirely (O.E.D.).

make (noun): 4.3.34: consort;
here, wife.

make (vb.): (i: 1.4.177:) mean;
(ii: 5.3.94:) prove; make
from: avoid; make good: put
into effect; make mouths:
practise facial expressions;
make up: accept a proposal;
make your loves: woo.

marjoram: sweet marjoram: a
medicinal herb.

mark (vb.): note.

mate and make: husband and
wife.

material (adj.): nourishing.

maugre: in spite of.

meads: meadows.

meaning: 1.2.166: intention.

means: 4.1.20: assets.

meet (adj.): fitting.

meiny: retinue.

memories: 4.7.7: reminders.

mercy: in mercy: at his mercy;
cry you mercy: I beg your
pardon.

mere: 2.4.85; 4.1.20: sheer, out-
right.

merits: deserts.

messes: meals.

metal: 1.1.68: (a) mettle, spirit;
(b) strong substance.

milk-livered: cowardly.

milky: mild, weak.

minces virtue: (perhaps) by a
mincing manner appears
virginal.

minikin: 3.6.43: (a) dainty;
(b) shrill.

minister: servant, agent.

miscarry: (i: 5.1.5:) come to
harm or death; (ii: 5.1.44:) die.

mischief: injury, harm.

miscreant: 1.1.160: (a) infidel;
(b) villain.

modest: (i: 2.4.24:) appropriate;
(ii: 4.7.5:) exact.

mo: more.

moiety: share.

monster (vb.): make monstrous
or inhuman.

moonshine: 1.2.5: month.

moral: 4.2.58: moralising.

morrow: morning.

mortality: 4.6.134: (a) death;
(b) human life.

mortified: deadened to pain.

mother: 2.4.54: lit. womb; here, hysteria.

motion: 2.1.49: fencer's thrust.

moulds: **Nature's moulds**: moulds that shape all natural forms.

mouths: **make mouths**: practise expressions.

move: 1.4.261: anger.

mow: grimace.

mutiny: strife.

mysteries: secret rites.

natural: 2.1.83: appropriately loving; **natural fool**: congenital fool.

Nature: 1.1.211; 1.2.1; 1.4.262; 2.2.50; 3.2.8; 4.6.135: goddess of the natural world.

nature: (i: 3.6.75; 4.6.86:) the natural order; (ii: 1.2.101, 107; 4.6.206:) human nature, human kind; (iii: 1.1.170, 234; 1.2.172; 1.5.28; 2.2.71, 93; 2.4.166; 4.2.32; 5.3.243:) character, disposition; (iv: 1.1.52; 2.4.173; 3.5.2; 3.7.84:) filial affection; (v: 2.4.103, 142, 261, 264; 3.2.48; 3.4.3, 67; 3.6.95; 4.4.12; 4.6.39; 4.7.15:) bodily constitution, natural life; (vi: 1.2.11:) instinctual sexuality; **wisdom of nature**: science.

naught: (noun:) nothing; (adj.) wicked.

naughty: wicked.

neat: trim, dandified.

necessity: poverty, neediness.

nether-stocks: stockings, coverings for the feet and lower legs.

nicely: scrupulously.

nighted: darkened (by blindness).

nightmare: 3.4.115: (a) female goblin; (b) devilish female incubus.

noises: **high noises**: 3.6.109: (a) serious reports; (b) important rumours.

nonny: 'meaningless refrain' (*O.E.D.*).

note: **take this note**: take note of this.

notice: 2.4.244: recognition.

notion: 1.4.215: intellect.

nuncle: 'mine uncle': dear master.

nursery: nursing, care.

object: (i: 1.1.213:) object of love; (ii: 2.3.17; 5.3.237:) spectacle.

óbservant (noun): watchful servant.

occasion: (i: 1.3.25:) opportunity for fault-finding; (ii: 2.1.119:) event.

o'erlooking: inspection.

o'erwatched: weary from lack of sleep.

offend: (i: 1.1.301:) harm; (ii: 1.2.40:) cause offence.

office: duty.

old: 3.7.99: normal.

on: (i: 1.2.117:) by; (ii: 5.3.101, 164, 245:) against; **on's**: of his.

opposite (noun): 5.3.43, 152: opponent.

orbs: 1.1.110: heavenly spheres: planets and stars.

ordinance: laws.

out: 1.1.31: away from home.

outface: defy.

out-jest: dispel by jesting.

out-paramour: have more mistresses than.

out-wall: exterior.

over-lusty: too vigorous.

overture: disclosure.

owe: 1.1.201; 1.4.111: own.

pack (noun): 5.3.18: cabal, clique.

pack (vb.): 2.4.76: depart.

packing: plotting.

pain: (i: 1.4.273:) trouble; (ii: 3.1.53:) effort.

pandar (pander): pimp.

part (vb.:) 1.2.23; 4.3.21: depart.

part (noun): 1.4.250: personal quality.

particular: personal, private; for his particular: as for himself.

party: (i: 2.1.26; 4.5.40; 4.6.250:) side (in a conflict): (ii: 3.5.9:) ally.

pass upon: pass judgement against.

pat: neat, neatly.

patience: self-control; readiness to endure.

pawn: 1.1.154: pledge to fight; pawn down: pledge.

peascod: pea-pod.

pell-mell: in wild promiscuity.

pelting: paltry.

pendulous: hanging overhead.

penning: handwriting.

perdu (Fr.): 4.7.35: (a) lost one, castaway; (b) sentry perilously placed.

perdy (from Fr. par Dieu): indeed.

perforce: necessarily.

period: 4.7.95; 5.3.203: (a) termination, climax; (b) full stop.

pew: seat.

physic: medical treatment.

piece (noun): 4.6.135: (a) masterpiece; (b) part.

piece (vb.): (i: 1.1.198:) combine; (ii: 3.6.2:) eke.

pight: resolved.

Pillicock: 3.4.73: (a) Mr Pillock; (b) penis.

Pillicock Hill: mons Veneris: Mount of Venus.

pinfold: pen for stray animals; in Lipsbury Pinfold: penned within the lips, teeth-gripped.

pity: 3.3.2: take pity on: aid.

place: (i: 1.1.170; 2.4.11; 5.3.65:) rank, station; (ii: 2.4.244:) residence.

placket: slit in petticoat or skirt.

plain: 3.1.39: complain.

plate (vb.): clothe in plate armour.

pleasant: 5.3.169: pleasure-giving.

pleasure: constant pleasure: settled preference.

plight (noun): pledge (of betrothal).

plight (vb.): (i: 1.1.278:) plait, fold; (ii: 3.4.117:) pledge, take an oath.

pluck: draw, pull.

point: 4.7.95: purpose, aim; at point: in readiness.

policy: 1.2.45: (a) established custom; (b) crafty device.

politician: trickster, schemer.

ponderous: weighty, substantial.

porridge: broth.

portable: endurable.
post (noun): courier.
post (vb.): ride speedily.
potency made good: power put into effect.
potential: powerful.
power: army, military force.
practice: trick, plot.
practise on: plot against.
prefer: promote.
pregnant: 2.1.75: compelling; **pregnant to**: 4.6.223: (a) penetrable by; (b) full of.
prescribed: limited.
present: 1.1.191: immediate.
presented: 2.3.11: displayed.
presently: immediately.
press-money: cash paid when a man is 'pressed' into military service.
pretence: 1.2.83; 1.4.65: intention.
pretty: (i: 1.4.89:) dear little; (ii: 1.5.31:) apt, neat; **pretty fellow**: fine fellow.
prevent: forestall.
prey: 3.4.89: preying, rapacity.
price: 1.1.196: (a) monetary dowry-value; (b) worth.
prick: 2.3.16: splinter.
prize (noun): (i: 2.1.119:) importance; (ii: 4.6.226:) person whose death earns a reward.
prize (vb.): estimate, value.
proclaimed: 2.3.1: publicly declared an outlaw; **proclaimed prize**: person whose death earns a proclaimed reward.
produce: exhibit.
profess: 1.4.11-12: (a) term one's profession; (b) claim to be.
promise: 1.2.138: assure.

proof: 2.3.13: evidence; **in proof**: to the test.
proper: (i: 1.1.17:) a) handsome; (b) seemly; (ii: 4.2.60:) characteristic.
property of blood: claims to blood-relationship.
propinquity: close kinship.
provoke: 4.4.13: cause, induce.
provoking merit: provocative sense of his own deserts.
publish: declare publicly.
pudder: turmoil.
puissant (Fr.): powerful, overpowering.
put on: (i: 1.4.195:) encourage; (ii: 2.1.98:) incite to; **put up**: stow, pocket.
quality: (i: 1.2.12, 33; 2.4.88, 91, 132:) character, nature; (ii: 5.3.110, 119:) rank.
quarrel (noun): 3.7.75; 5.3.57: contention, cause.
queasy: delicate, difficult.
question: (i: 4.3.24:) response; (ii: 5.1.31; 5.3.59:) matter, topic; (iii: 5.3.34:) discussion; **come to question**: provoke argument; **queasy question**: risky nature.
questrist: searcher.
quicken: regain life.
quit: (i: 2.1.30:) acquit; (ii: 3.7.85:) avenge.
rage (noun): 4.4.19; 4.7.78: madness.
raise: 2.4.42: rouse.
rake up: cover up with soil or sand.
rank: (i: 1.4.191:) gross, excessive; (ii: 4.3.3:) coarsely luxuriant.

ravish: tear, snatch.

raze: erase.

reason (noun): 1.4.325: argument.

reason (vb.): (i: 1.2.100:) explain; (ii: 2.4.259; 5.1.28:) argue about.

recreant: traitor.

reeking: steaming with sweat.

regard: (i: 1.1.238:) consideration; (ii: 1.4.252:) detail.

rein: **hard rein**: harsh treatment.

relish (vb.): enjoy.

remediate: remedial.

remember: 1.4.62: remind; **thyself remember**: recall penitently thy past sins.

remorse: 4.2.73: pity.

remotion: 2.4.109: (a) aloofness; (b) departure.

remove (noun): 2.4.4: departure.

renege: deny.

repeal: recall into favour.

reposal: placing.

reservation: (i: 1.1.132:) retention for oneself; (ii: 2.4.247:) stipulated right.

reserve (vb.): retain.

resolution: freedom from doubt.

resolve me: make clear to me.

rest: **set my rest on**: 1.1.122–3: (a) commit myself finally to; (b) repose finally in.

retention: 5.3.48: imprisonment.

retreat: 5.2.4, S.D.: (a) trumpet-call ordering retreat; (b) noises of retreat.

reverb: echo.

rival (vb.): compete.

rive: split open.

rogue: 4.7.39: vagrant.

roguish: vagabond-like.

round: 1.4.49: plain-spoken.

rub: 2.2.148: impede.

rude: rough and unmannerly.

ruffle: (i: 2.4.296:) bluster; (ii: 3.7.40:) snatch.

sa, sa (Fr. ça, ça): hunting-cry to urge dogs: hence, 'come on'.

safe: 1.4.193: sure; **the safer sense**: sanity.

sallet: salad.

salt: 4.6.195: tears.

sampire (samphire): aromatic plant used in pickles.

sapient: wise.

saucy: insolent.

savour (noun): character.

savour (vb.): relish.

saw: 2.2.154: proverb.

say: 5.3.142: evidence.

scant (vb.): (i: 1.1.276; 2.4.135; 3.2.67:) withhold; (ii: 2.4.170:) reduce.

scape: escape.

scattered: 3.1.31: disunited.

scurvy: 4.6.171: scabby; hence, nasty.

Scythian: nomadic Asian warrior.

second (noun): supporter.

secret (noun): 4.4.15: remedy known to doctors only.

sect: party, faction.

sectary astronomical: devotee of astrology.

secure (vb.): make over-confident.

seize upon (or **on**): take legal possession of.

self: 1.1.68; 4.3.34: same.

sennet: fanfare.

sequent: consequent.

serviceable: obsequiously diligent.

set (vb.): 1.4.114: wager.

settling: calming down.

Seven Stars: 1.5.31: (a) the Plough; (b) Pleiades.

shake a beard: challenge to a fight.

shealed: shelled, emptied.

shiver: 4.6.51: shatter.

shorten: 4.7.9: frustrate.

show (noun): 3.6.103: appearance.

show (vb.): 1.4.230, 254; 4.2.60; 4.6.14: appear.

shrill-gorged: shrill-voiced.

silly-ducking: foolishly-bowing.

simple (noun): medicine from a single herb.

simple (adj.): 4.6.152: (a) common; (b) humble; (c) mentally weak.

simular of: pretender to.

sinew: nerve.

single virtue: unaided merit.

sith: since.

sizes: 2.4.170: allowances.

skill: 4.7.66: mental ability.

slack (vb.): be neglectful of.

slack (adv.): **come slack of**: fall short of.

slave (vb.): treat contemptuously.

slipshod: shod in slippers.

sliver: split.

smilet: little smile.

smooth (vb.): 2.2.70: aid, encourage.

smug: trim, spruce.

snow (fig.): 4.6.119: frigid chastity.

snuff: (i: 3.1.26:) huff, resentment; (ii: 4.6.39:) candle-end.

soiled: 4.6.122: fed with fresh green fodder; hence, lively.

something: 1.1.20; 3.5.3: somewhat.

son: 1.1.40, 41: son-in-law.

soothe: 3.4.170: humour.

sop o'th'moonshine: 2.2.29: (a: perhaps) bread-sop so perforated that the moon shines through it; (b: perhaps) bread-sop soaked in moonlit blood.

sophisticated: adulterated, corrupted.

sot: fool.

sound (vb.): assess.

sovereign (adj.): overpowering.

space: (i: 1.1.55:) scope; (ii: 1.1.80; 4.6.271:) extent; (iii: 5.3.54:) time.

speculation: observer.

speed (vb.): 1.2.19: succeed; **speed you**: may God give you success.

spherical: of some planet or cosmic sphere.

spill: 3.2.8: (a) destroy; (b) disperse.

spleen: malice, ill-temper.

spoil: 5.3.277: ruin.

square of sense: regulator of meaning: the mind.

squiny: squint, peer.

squire-like: like a vassal.

stand: 2.1.39: act as; **stand in hard cure**: will be hard to heal; **stand on**: obliges.

star-blasting: blighting by an

adverse star.

start (noun): 1.1.296: outburst.

start (vb.): 4.3.31: move abruptly.

starved: 5.3.25: dead.

state: (i: 1.1.49; 5.1.22:) government, rule; (ii: 1.1.148; 2.4.107:) kingly power; (iii: 1.2.141; 3.1.25:) kingdom; (iv: 2.2.163:) situation; (v: 2.4.144:) condition of mind; (vi: 5.1.68: a) exalted position; (b) state of affairs.

stellèd: 3.7.59: (a) starry; (b) fixed.

stiff: 4.6.279: stubborn.

still (adv.): always, constantly.

still-soliciting: 1.1.230: (a) continually begging; (b) silently soliciting.

stomach: full-flowing stomach: bellyful of rage.

stone: 5.3.261: reflective or transparent mineral (e.g. mica) used as a mirror.

straight: (i: 1.3.26; 2.4.34; 3.6.20; 5.3.286:) immediately; (ii: 5.3.278:) plainly.

strain: 5.3.41: (a) quality; (b) lineage.

strained: 1.1.168: unnatural, forced.

stretch: 2.2.99: strain.

strings of life: heart-strings.

sub-contracted: betrothed to one man while married to another.

subscription: submission.

succeed: 1.2.138: ensue.

success: 5.3.193: outcome.

suffer: (i: 1.2.50:) endure;

(ii: 4.2.44:) allow

sufferance: suffering.

suit (noun): entreaty.

suited: clothed.

sulph'rous: explosive (sulphur being used in gunpowder).

summoner: officer who summoned offenders to an ecclesiastical court.

sumpter: pack-horse; hence, drudge.

superfluous: pampered.

superflux: surplus.

super-serviceable: offering excessive service.

support: (i: 1.4.252:) uphold; (ii: 5.3.196:) endure.

surfeit: sickness resulting from excess.

sustaining: 4.4.6: (a) supporting life; (b) supporting weeds.

sway (noun): government, direction; **i'th'sway**: guided by.

sway (vb.): govern.

swear: 1.1.160: invoke.

sweet marjoram: a medicinal herb.

S'Withold: Saint Withold.

sword: 5.3.33: swordsman.

taint: 1.1.220: discredit.

taken: 1.4.317: overtaken by harm.

take that of me: learn that from me.

take upon's: 5.3.16: (a) bear, take on; (b) claim to know.

taking (noun): (i: 2.3.5:) capture; (ii: 3.4.57:) bewitchment; (iii: 4.6.29:) acceptance; **taking off**: murder.

taking (adj.): 2.4.159: noxious.

tame: 4.6.221: humbly submissive.

tart (adj.): disagreeable.

taste: 1.2.44: test.

tax with: accuse of.

teem: bear children.

tell: 2.4.53; 3.2.91: count.

temper (noun): 1.5.41: mental balance, sanity.

temper (vb.): 1.4.291: soften.

temperance: self-control.

tender-hefted: softly-shaped, gentle.

tender of: solicitude for.

tend upon: serve.

thick: 3.2.7: solid.

thing: 1.5.46: penis.

thin helm: 4.7.36: light helmet; hence, (a) hair; (b) balding or thin-haired crown of head.

thought-executing: 3.2.4: (a) acting speedily as thought; (b) mind-destroying.

thrill: pierce.

threading: penetrating arduously.

throughly: thoroughly.

throw: 1.4.114: risk at a throw of dice.

thwart (adj.): perverse.

time's plague: evil of our time.

tithing: parish, district.

toad-spotted: marked with infamy, as a toad with spots.

together: 1.2.149: without intermission.

Tom o'Bedlam: see Bedlam.

top (vb.): 1.2.21; 5.3.206: rise above, surpass.

touch: (i: 2.4.271; 5.3.231:) imbue; (ii: 4.6.83:) censure; (iii: 5.1.25:) concern.

toward: 2.1.10; 3.3.18; 4.6.209: impending.

trade: activity, business.

transport (vb.): 1.4.209: carry away emotionally.

treacher: traitor.

trick: 4.6.106: characteristic.

trill (vb.): trickle.

troop with: accompany.

troth: her troth plight: make her solemn promise.

trundle-tail: dog with long curly tail.

trunk: body.

tucket: trumpet-call.

tune (fig.): 4.3.39: mood.

turn: (i: 3.2.67:) become disordered; (ii: 4.6.23:) become giddy.

tyke: mongrel.

unaccommodated: without civilised accessories, e.g. clothes.

unbolted: unsifted; hence, unmitigated.

unbonneted: hatless.

unburthened: unburdened.

unconstant: sudden and erratic.

understanding: in understanding: from knowledge.

ungracious: wicked (devoid of divine grace).

unhappily: unfortunately.

unhappy: unlucky.

unkind: lacking in natural affection.

unkindness: absence of natural affection between parents and children.

unnatural: (i: 3.1.38:) contrary to the laws of nature; (ii: 2.1.49; 2.4.273; 3.3.1, 6:) unfilial.

unnaturalness: lack of the

affection that should exist
among blood-relatives.

unpossessing: incapable of in-
heriting the father's possessions.

unprovided: unarmed.

unstate myself: surrender my
rank and fortune.

untented: 1.4.287: too deep for
cleansing; hence, incurable.
(A 'tent' is a cleansing probe.)

Ursa Major: the Great Bear
constellation.

use: (i: 1.3.20; 2.2.10; 4.6.191;
5.3.44:) treat; (ii: 1.4.160:) be
in the habit of doing.

usurer: money-lender.

usurp: falsely claim or retain.

vain: 4.2.61: (a) futile; (b) silly.

validity: value.

varlet: 2.2.25; 2.4.182:
(a) menial; (b) rogue.

vassal: slave.

vaunt-couriers: fore-runners.

very: (i: 1.3.27:) exact;
(ii: 1.4.65:) real.

vex: disturb.

vild (vile): (i: 3.2.71:) seemingly
worthless; (ii: 3.4.138; 3.7.81;
4.2.38, 47; 4.6.279:) loathsome.

villain: (i: 3.7.76; 4.6.246:) serf,
menial; (ii: 3.7.85:) rogue.

virtue: 4.4.16: (a) healing
power; (b) healing herb.

volk (dial.): folk.

vor' (dial.): warrant, warn.

vulgar: 4.6.210: commonly
known and spoken of.

vurther (dial.): further.

wage: (i: 1.1.155:) stake in
wager; hence, risk;
(ii: 2.4.204:) contend.

wagtail (fig.): 2.2.62: obsequious
person (repeatedly bowing).

wake: 3.6.72: parish festival
with sports and games.

walk: 4.7.83: withdraw.

wall-newt: lizard.

want: lack.

wanton (noun): friskily way-
ward creature.

wanton (adj.): playfully unre-
strained.

warped: twisted.

watch: (i: 2.2.149; 4.7.35:)
remain sleepless; (ii: 2.1.20:)
be on the lookout;
o'erwatched: weary from
lack of sleep.

wawl: howl, wail

weal: state, society.

web: **the web and the pin**:
cataract of the eye.

weeds: 4.7.7: clothes.

weight: 5.3.322: burden of
sorrow.

well-favoured: pleasant in
appearance.

what: (i: 3.6.112:) whatever;
(ii: 4.6.48, 220; 5.3.118, 124,
163:) who; (iii: 5.3.98:) who-
ever.

whelked: twisted and convo-
luted like a whelk.

where: (i: 1.2.78:) whereas;
(ii: 3.7.9:) to whom;
(iii: 4.5.10:) wherever.

whistling: **worth the whistling**:
4.2.29: (a) worth calling for;
(b) worth co-operating with.

white: 3.4.112: ready for
harvesting.

whoremaster: pimp.

whoreson: son of a whore.

wide: 4.7.50: astray.

wide-skirted: extensive.

wield: 1.1.54: express.

wind into him: gain his confidence.

windowed: with window-like holes.

wits: five wits: mental faculties.

withal: 1.2.98: therewith, with that.

word: (i: 3.4.176:) watchword, motto; (ii: 4.6.92:) password.

worship: honour.

worth: 4.4.10: wealth.

worthy (vb.): make a hero of.

worthy (adj.): 5.3.177: noble.

write: 5.3.36: sign yourself.

yield: 4.6.44: consent.

yoke-fellow: equal partner.

zir (dial.): sir.

zwaggered (dial.): 'swaggered': bullied.